Plays by
Stephen Belber

Broadway Play Publishing Inc
New York
BroadwayPlayPub.com

Cover photo: Jemal Countess

First printing: November 2020
I S B N: 978-0-88145-869-5

Book design: Marie Donovan
Typeface: Palatino

TAPE

TAPE was originally developed and workshopped at the Access Theater (Jacqueline Christy, Artistic Director) in New York City on 6 May 1999. The cast and creative contributors were as follows:

VINCE.. Dominic Fumusa
JON .... Josh Stamberg
AMY .... Phoebe Jonas

Director .... Steven Pickering
Set design .... Charles Kirby
Lighting design .... Tyler Micoleau
Stage manager .... Susanna Harris

TAPE premiered in the 2000 Humana Festival of New American Plays at Actors Theatre of Louisville (Jon Jory, Artistic Director) in Louisville, Kentucky, on 29 February 2000. The cast and creative contributors were as follows:

VINCE... Dominic Fumusa
JON .... Stephen Kunken
AMY ....Erica Yoder

Director.. Brian Jucha
Set design..Paul Owen
Lighting design .... Greg Sullivan
Sound design..Martin Desjardins
Costume design...Suttirat Larlarb
Stage manager ....Charles M Turner III
Dramaturg..................................... Michael Bigelow Dixon

TAPE premiered in New York City at the Jose Quintero Theater on January 17, 2002. It was presented by Naked Angels Theater Company (Ilana Levine and Sherri Kotimsky, Producers; Tim Ransom, Artistic Director). The cast and creative contributors were as follows:

VINCE... Dominic Fumusa
JON .... Josh Stamberg
AMY .... Alison West

Director ....Geoffrey Nauffts
Set design ....George Xenos
Lighting design ....Greg Macpherson
Sound design.. Roger Raines
Costume design... Sarah Beers
Stage manager...Peggy Samuels

CHARACTERS & SETTING

VINCE, *beat-up jeans, no shoes, maybe a tank top T-shirt; lovable, self-destructive type.*

JON, *dressed casually but well, with a degree of "hip" thrown in—V-neck sweater, no T-shirt; retro, perfectly fitting jeans, worn leather jacket, brown leather shoes.*

AMY, *dressed casually—the way a young attorney might be on a Friday night.*

Place: A Motel 6 motel room, Lansing, Michigan.

Time: The present.

AUTHOR'S NOTE

TAPE may be performed in one of two ways:

First option is to perform the play with just the prologue and the play itself. In this instance, the play will end with Vince and Jon alone in the motel room, unable to say anything to one another as lights fade.

Second option is to include the prologue and the epilogue. In this case, at play's finish, we would cross fade into the epilogue's three monologues. In this instance, the play would end at the close of Amy's monolgue.

That being said, the play may also be performed without the prologue or the epilogue. Or it could be performed with the prologue and only Amy's monologue from the epilogue, (thus cutting Vince and Jon's monologues).

special thanks and gratitude to
Jeremy Norton, Josh Stamberg and Dominic Fumusa

(A Motel 6 motel room, Lansing, Michigan. Music—perhaps Eddie Cochrane—plays loudly. VINCE, twenty-eight, stands alone at the sink outside the bathroom pouring the contents of a can of Schlitz into the sink with one hand while holding and drinking from a second can of Schlitz in the other. When the first can is empty, he chucks it casually onto the floor. He opens another can from a six-pack which rests on the sink and repeats the action. When it is empty, he tosses it across the room. At about this time, he finishes the beer he is drinking and throws it towards the T V. He opens another beer to drink and another one to empty. But first, he takes off his blue jeans and throws them on the bed. He returns to his task of emptying beers. Eventually, there is a knock on the door. He finishes emptying the beer and chucks it onto one of the beds as he goes to answer. He takes a moment to muss his hair, then opens...JON, twenty-eight, enters. They hug. Several seconds)

VINCE: Hey, man!

JON: Hey, Vince!

(JON and VINCE hug—warm, genuine, an obviously old friendship.)

VINCE: Welcome to my palazzio!

JON: This is great, man!

VINCE: Yeah!—

JON: This is great!—

VINCE: How are you?

JON: Can't complain.

VINCE: Cool!

JON: Totally. It is, I'm very psyched.

VINCE: You should be, Jonny, it's a great thing.

JON: Thanks, man. Thanks.

(JON *and* VINCE *hug again.*)

VINCE: You know what else?

JON: What?

VINCE: It's great to be alive!

JON: Totally! *(Beat)* What's up?

VINCE: Not much.

JON: You're not dressed.

VINCE: Lay off.

JON: It's not that I don't like it—

VINCE: But—?

JON: But nothing.

VINCE: So—?

JON: So nothing—

VINCE: Okay!

JON: Okay.

VINCE: Excellent!

JON: Fine. *(Beat; a smile.)* I swear to God you get stranger each year.

VINCE: You look good, Jon.

(JON *enters the room more fully now, looking around.*)

JON: Where's Leah?

VINCE: Didn't make the trip.

JON: Why not?

VINCE: We broke up.

JON: Shut up.

VINCE: I'm serious—

JON: Shut up—

VINCE: I'm serious—

JON: You broke up?!

VINCE: We broke up.

JON: Why?—

VINCE: Complicated—

JON: Why?—

VINCE: She didn't like the way I dress.

JON: Don't joke—

VINCE: I'm not.

JON: What happened?

VINCE: I get stranger each year.

JON: Vince—

VINCE: She thinks I'm a dick. *(Pause)* She sends apologies for not coming. She says she's sure it'll go well.

JON: *(Pause)* I don't believe it.

VINCE: I'm serious, man, she does—

JON: Why did you break up?

VINCE: I don't know.

(Silence)

JON: I'm sorry, man.

VINCE: Me too.

JON: *(Beat)* Is it permanent?

VINCE: Permanent as a dead horse, amigo.

JON: *(Beat)* Did you do something?

VINCE: Why do you say that?

JON: Because I know you.

VINCE: *You* think I'm a dick—

JON: No, it's just that I know that you occasionally have a tendency to *act* in a phallic fashion.

VINCE: I'm not like that anymore.

JON: What—you're not a dick?

VINCE: See what I mean?

JON: I'm just asking what happened.

VINCE: Lots of things.

JON: Like?—

VINCE: Like she thinks I'm reckless.

JON: In general?

VINCE: Yes.

JON: *(Pause)* Were you at all *specifically* reckless recently?

VINCE: Not particularly specifically.

JON: Be honest—

VINCE: I am.

JON: Did you fuck around?

VINCE: No!

JON: Vince?—

VINCE: I didn't!

JON: So what happened?

Vince. She says I have violent tendencies.

JON: ...Oh boy...

VINCE: I never touched her, Jon.

JON: I didn't say you did.

VINCE: It's just that she *thinks* I have "unresolved issues which occasionally manifest themselves in potentially violent ways." *(Beat)* What?

JON: I think it's fair to say she has a point.

VINCE: No one's saying she doesn't have a point.

JON: So—?

VINCE: So she has to break up with me?

JON: She's probably scared.

VINCE: Of what? I never threatened her.

JON: You present a threatening appearance.

VINCE: Dude, we've been together *three* years!

JON: So?

VINCE: So you think she'd be used to it by now!

JON: It's a tricky one, Vin.

VINCE: What're you talking about?

JON: I'm just saying, it's tricky. Women these days have no reason to hang around potentially violent guys. It's not an attractive quality to them anymore. Too many other guys out there with *resolved* violent tendencies.

VINCE: So I'm just out of fashion?

JON: Don't be a fool—

VINCE: Don't be a politically correct fuck!—

JON: I'm not, I'm telling you that you're an idiot if you think chicks are gonna put up with your bullshit.

VINCE: What bullshit?—

JON: Like playing rough—

VINCE: I didn't play rough with her.

JON: Vince—

VINCE: What?—

JON: I love you—

VINCE: Good—

JON: —but c'mon.

VINCE: What?—

JON: You don't *not* play rough.

VINCE: I totally *do* not play rough.

JON: You're swarthy.

VINCE: That's a stereotype.

JON: True.

VINCE: Bigot.

JON: I can't be a bigot—I'm a Jew.

VINCE: I know plenty of Jewish bigots.

JON: Who?

VINCE: Irving Berlin.

JON: *(Beat)* Okay, let's move to the next subject—

VINCE: Fine.

JON: I'm sorry you guys broke up. Really. I'm sorry for you both.

VINCE: *(Aside)* Don't be sorry for *that* bitch…

JON: Fine, I'm just sorry for you. Next subject.

(Beat)

VINCE: She says if I get my act together, stick with the meetings and stop being a dick, she might consider talking to me again.

(JON gives a slight kick to one of the empty beer cans on the floor.)

JON: Good. *(Beat)* Should we get some dinner?

VINCE: I gotta wait for a call.

JON: From who?

VINCE: None of your business.

JON: Leah?

VINCE: *(Indignant.)* No.

JON: …O-kay.

(Silence)

VINCE: *(Sulky.)* So are you ready for tomorrow?

JON: You're mad.

VINCE: I'm not mad—

JON: You're allowed to be—

VINCE: I'm not mad. I'll find someone else.

JON: It's true—

VINCE: Who *appreciates* my dark side.

JON: Exactly. *(Pause)* But the thing is, if you could maybe find a way to learn something from this, then you won't have as *large* of a dark side.

VINCE: *(Beat)* Learn what?

JON: Learn to deal with some of your violent desires.

VINCE: *(Skeptical)* How?

JON: By acknowledging them, by making some type of truce with yourself where you're not always in constant battle to prove your integrity, or your self-worth or whatever it is that you think nobody gets about you.

VINCE: I don't think there's anything to get about me. I'm a simple man.

JON: Yeah, but your idea of manhood is putting on Eddie Cochrane and screwing your girl. It's not like that anymore. Women want other things.

VINCE: Like what?

JON: I don't know. *(Beat)*…Enya.

VINCE: *(Beat; unconvinced.)* Yeah.

(Silence)

JON: Vince—

VINCE: So where're you staying?

JON: *(Pause)* They got me over at the Radisson in town.

VINCE: *NICE!!*

JON: Yeah, it is.

VINCE: Lansing Film Festival!

JON: Yeah, that and Cannes.

VINCE: Still, it's a good gig.

JON: It's a good cheap thrill.

VINCE: Why do you have to dump on it? —It's a good gig.

JON: Because I have big expectations. I spent two years on this film, I want it to be in a theater near you.

VINCE: *(Re: window.)* It is.

JON: Yeah, but you had to come out to the middle of fucking Michigan to be there. For *one* screening, for which I'm getting paid a whopping five hundred bucks.

VINCE: Yeah, but all you need is for one guy from—whatever—from Disney to be there tomorrow—he likes it—boom, next thing you know, you're directing *Free Willy Four.*

JON: Starring David Hasselhoff.

VINCE: Hey—

JON: Hey—

VINCE: Hey—

JON: Hey. *(Beat)* Dude, I'm starving.

VINCE: What time is it?

JON: *(Re: watch)* Quarter of.

VINCE: You wanna a beer?

JON: Aren't you supposed to be getting your act together?

VINCE: I'll do it when I get back.

JON: See, this is what she's talking about—

VINCE: Jon—if I wanted to hang out with my mother… right?

JON: Well put.

VINCE: What Leah doesn't know won't hurt her. *(He carefully and rather deliberately reaches into his bag. Beat.)*

JON: Whattayou got goin' on in that bag, Vince?

VINCE: Beer.

JON: How much?

VINCE: Lot.

(VINCE tosses JON a beer, then opens one for himself.)

JON: I don't know why I said you had violent tendencies.

VINCE: Why?—

JON: Warm beer, boxers, Motel 6. Who needs Betty Ford?

VINCE: We can't *all* be at the Radisson.

JON: Hey—you know, if you wanna stay with me—

VINCE: No.

JON: Seriously, I thought you'd be with Leah, that's why I didn't offer earlier—

VINCE: It's not a problem—

JON: It's *not* a problem—they gave me a double; eleventh floor overlooking a park—

VINCE: No, man, you probably wanna get laid.

JON: *(Pause)* That's true.

VINCE: It's your big weekend, chicks are gonna flock to you.

JON: You're right.

VINCE: I'll be fine here.

JON: Cool.

VINCE: Should I twist your arm?

JON: Yeah. More.

VINCE: Schmuck—

JON: Prick—

VINCE: Putz—

JON: Suck-ass. *(Beat)* I appreciate you coming out here. Seriously. We've come a long way.

VINCE: Since—?

JON: I dunno. High school.

VINCE: You think?

JON: Some of us. *(Pause)* Dude, I'm totally giving you shit.

VINCE: No but you're right—

JON: No I'm not—

VINCE: You are, face it—

JON: I'm right only in that I think you can do better than you are.

VINCE: Why?—

JON: Because I believe in you. If I didn't, we wouldn't still be friends *and* I wouldn't be able to say that to you.

VINCE: Why not?

JON: Because it sounds totally pretentious.

VINCE: You're right—

JON: But the thing is—I mean it. I'm sorry but it's true. It's like this thing with Leah—if it *is* permanent, then you should view it as an opportunity to change—

VINCE: Change *what?*

JON: I don't know—find a new job, new way of doing things—

VINCE: I like my job.

JON: What *is* your job?

VINCE: Volunteer firefighter.

JON: I know, but how do you make your money?

VINCE: Lay off.

JON: I'm just saying—

VINCE: What?

JON: —it's immature.

VINCE: *You* try doing it—

JON: That's not the point—

VINCE: Besides, the majority of my clients happen to be over fifty. If that's not mature, I'm baffled as to what is.

JON: Private dope delivery to ex-hippies does not a mature man make, Vince. It's not that different than standing on the corner selling to teenagers—

VINCE: Why're you lecturing me?

JON: I'm not, I'm just pointing things out—

VINCE: Such as?—

JON: Such as I think you can do better.

VINCE: Than what?—

JON: Than pissing your life away. You're a smart guy, why're you still dealing drugs?

VINCE: *Because* I'm smart. If I was dumb, I would've gotten caught by now. Besides—I'm a firefighter.

JON: You *deal* to the fire *chief*, Vince!

VINCE: He *needs* me!

JON: That's not the point—

VINCE: Why is what you do better?!

JON: Why is what I do better?

VINCE: Yeah.

JON: *(Pause)* What I'm *trying* to do is better because it's an attempt at figuring things out. I would like to, eventually, become good enough at it to the point where I can contribute to a larger debate about why this country is so fucked up. I would like to try and examine why it is that a fifty-whatever-year-old fire chief feels the need to get stoned every night. What is it about life in America that's driving that urge in him?

VINCE: He *likes* it?

JON: Fine, but then there's something slightly wrong with the fact that someone with that type of responsibility is constantly *high*. There's maybe some sort of symbolism there worth examining.

VINCE: His firehouse happens to have the best record in the city—

JON: Vince—if my house was on fire, I wouldn't want his high ass anywhere *near* it—

VINCE: You're such a fucking bigot!—

JON: The guy has a good record because he's *lucky!*—

VINCE: Says who?

JON: It's obvious! He's living a big, luck-driven lie!

VINCE: What're you—high?

JON: I'm serious—

VINCE: You're making movies about people who rob *Popeye's Fried Chicken!*—

JON: I'm telling a story which aims to resonate the notion of where our society's headed if we're not careful. The only reason it sounds pompous is because I haven't fully honed my skills yet.

VINCE: It doesn't sound pompous, it sounds like you're talking out your ass—

JON: Why?

VINCE: Because you have no idea where society is headed. You're just like everybody else—you're following the latest trend which you hope will get you laid until the trend switches to something else, at which point you'll drop the old one and make a movie about—whatever—like turtles that get caught in fishing nets. Starring...*Cindy* Hasselhoff. *(Beat)* His niece.

JON: *(Wounded...)* You don't like my work?

VINCE: I like it like I like a shot of whiskey first thing in the morning—it's good for about ten minutes, then I want my coffee.

JON: *(Beat)* Wow.

VINCE: What?

JON: Did I say something to piss you off? Or is it that you're just a dick?

VINCE: Both.

JON: Good to see that you're finally admitting it.

VINCE: Unlike some of us.

JON: What—that *I'm* a dick?

VINCE: Ah—yeah.

JON: When?

VINCE: I'm speaking figuratively.

JON: When was I figuratively a dick?

VINCE: High school.

JON: I was too shy to be a dick in high school.

VINCE: Oh I think you held your own.

JON: That's because *everyone's* a dick in high school, Vince. It's the white-male-football-playing prerogative. The trick is to evolve into something else once you're out.

VINCE: Jon, you're wearing two-hundred-dollar shoes.

JON: First of all, that's not true—

VINCE: One-fifty.

JON: I'm less shy than in high school.

VINCE: So you're an *overt* dick?

JON: No, actually, I'm a thoughtful person who wears nice shoes—

VINCE: And is occasionally full of shit.

JON: Is there something I'm not doing that you want me to do, Vince?

VINCE: I don't want you to do anything.

JON: No? —Because it seems like I'm being asked to do something by a twenty-eight-year-old pot dealer who refuses to progress with the rest of the world—which would be okay if it were a legitimate *rebellion* instead of just some lonely guy hanging out in his boxer shorts acting like a potentially violent dick!

VINCE: *(Beat)* You wanna get high?

JON: No.

VINCE: C'mon, Jon, get high—

JON: I'm not getting high—

VINCE: Why—only violent dicks get high?—

JON: No—

VINCE: So let's get high—

JON: I'm *not* getting high—

VINCE: *I* am! (*He goes into his duffel bag and carefully and deliberately searches around.*)

JON: Whattayou got goin' on in that bag, Vince?

VINCE: Pot.

JON: How much?

VINCE: A *lot.* (*He produces a very well-rolled joint, lights up and takes a large hit…*) Primo Levi…

(VINCE *then offers it to* JON, *who refuses…but then, after extreme and exaggerated efforts by* VINCE, *relents and accepts. They smoke in silence…*)

JON: (*Muttering*) Motherfucker…. (*He smokes, then raises his hands in mock celebration.*) High School!…

VINCE: (*Beats*) You know who's out here?

JON: Where?

VINCE: Here. Lansing.

JON: Who?

VINCE: Amy Randall.

JON: (*Pause*) Really?

VINCE: Yep. I heard that from Tracy about two years ago, then when you got this thing, I looked her up on the Net, and she's out here. She's like…an assistant county prosecutor or something.

JON: Did you call her?

VINCE: (*Pause*) I thought about it.

JON: You should, especially now that Leah's…

VINCE: Out of the picture?

JON: Yeah.

VINCE: Yeah.

JON: *(Pause)* I wonder if she's still…

VINCE: Hot?

JON: Yeah.

VINCE: That's not a very politically appropriate way to think about women, Jon.

JON: Okay—here's the thing with being appropriate: It's better to try and do that than to be a *complete* asshole. The choice to respect people is actually a *good* one, despite people like you who insist on calling fat people "fat" to their face.

VINCE: What if they're fat?

JON: If they're fat they probably already *realize* it without your having to remind them. It basically has to do with having a couple *manners*.

VINCE: Is that what it is?

JON: That's it.

VINCE: So why'd you ask if she was hot?

JON: Because she is. Was. It's not a bad word. If the word is essentially a compliment, then saying it isn't bad manners. Human beings like to be called attractive. I'm not labeling Amy Randall anything she doesn't already know. And I'm sure she's smart, too.

VINCE: Well if we call her and she weighs three hundred and twenty pounds, then I think we should go up to her and say, "Gee, we're really glad we dated you in high school instead of now because in high school you were really hot and now…well, I'm sure you already *realize* about now."

JON: You know what, Vince? —Why don't you shut up for awhile.

VINCE: Oh I see—I made a point so now I have to shut up?

JON: No, it's that you like being rude for the sake of it; either that or you do it to prove that nobody can *make* you be nice. Either way, it gets tiresome. And the thing is, you and I don't see each other often enough to make worthwhile this little competition for "who's more authentic." It's not about that anymore. Okay? We should just accept the fact that we're a little different from each other, and let the friendship go from there.

VINCE: "Accept the fact that we're a little different from each other"?

JON: Yeah.

VINCE: *(Pause...)* Would you like to make me?

JON: Make you what?

VINCE: Make me "accept that fact."

JON: No.

VINCE: Why not?

JON: 'Cause it's stupid.

VINCE: No it's not—

JON: Yes it is—

VINCE: No it's not because how else will I know that you're different?

JON: You'll just have to trust me.

VINCE: No. Prove it.

JON: Or else what?

VINCE: *(Matter of fact)* I kick your ass.

JON: *(Pause)* I guess this means you're potentially violent.

VINCE: *(Quiet menace)* Only when it comes to you, Jon.

JON: *(Beat)* Funny how you get this way every time we talk about Amy Randall.

VINCE: No I don't.

JON: I don't even think you realize it, Vince.

VINCE: Fuck off.

JON: Okay, you know what?—I'm outta here—

VINCE: Fuck off—

JON: Thanks for coming—

VINCE: Fuck off—

JON: Vincent.

VINCE: Fuck *you*, Jon!—

JON: Look—I'm sorry you still feel bad about Amy Randall, and that every time you get stoned and drunk around me this comes up. But it was ten years ago; I've explained to you a million times that I felt that it was okay for me to be with her because you guys had broken up, and that I now have a better understanding as to the *fragility* of human emotions—especially those belonging to swarthy Italian-Americans like yourself— and thus if the situation arose again today, I wouldn't let what happened happen. But these things *do* happen, especially in high school, and I'm sorry I hurt your feelings.

VINCE: *(Pause)* That's not what I'm talking about.

JON: What're you talking about?

VINCE: I'm talking about what happened.

JON: So am I.

VINCE: So what happened?

JON: We slept together.

VINCE: How?

JON: What do you mean?

VINCE: How did you sleep together?

JON: Okay—so now this is about that?

VINCE: Isn't it?

JON: Is it?

VINCE: *You* tell *me.*

JON: We slept together.

VINCE: How?

JON: You *know* how.

VINCE: No, actually, I don't. I have an idea, but I don't *know* because we've never actually *talked* about it. We've *laughed* about it; we thought it was kinda *funny,* but you've never exactly *told* me what happened.

JON: So what do you wanna know?

VINCE: I wanna know what happened.

JON: We slept together.

VINCE: How?

JON: What do you mean "how"?

VINCE: *How!*

JON: You have to be more specific, Vince.

VINCE: In what fashion did you sleep with her?

JON: We had sex.

VINCE: And—?

JON: And that was it.

VINCE: Was it good sex?

JON: I've had better since.

VINCE: Was it fun?

JON: It was all right.

VINCE: Was it on the rough side?

JON: Hard to say. We were both drunk.

VINCE: Did you rape her?

JON: *(Beat... Thinks he's joking)* No.

VINCE: Kind of?

JON: No!

VINCE: Was it like date rape?

JON: "*Like* date rape"?

VINCE: Did you "kind of" force her to have sex with you?

JON: No!!

(Silence)

VINCE: Jon?

JON: I'm not sure what you want me to say, Vince.

VINCE: I want you to tell me what happened. *You're* a filmmaker—lay out the scene for me; show me the dailies.

JON: Can we talk about this sometime when you're not high?

VINCE: Maybe the only reason I'm high is so that *you* get high so that for once you can tell me the truth instead of changing the subject.

JON: *(Beat)* Yes, it was a little rough. Which is obviously something that doesn't make me proud.

VINCE: *(Beat)* Did you ever talk to her after that?

JON: No.

VINCE: Why not?

JON: Because I wouldn't know what to say to her. I'm a completely different person than I was then.

VINCE: Maybe she is too.

JON: May-be.

VINCE: Maybe she's fat.

JON: That's really not funny.

VINCE: I didn't say it was. *(Beat)* Does anyone else know what happened?

JON: *I* didn't tell anyone.

VINCE: Maybe you should.

JON: I don't actually consider it a crime, Vince. It was not a good thing; it was morally somewhat questionable and I wish it hadn't happened, but I don't think it's the type of thing where I need to turn myself into the police ten years later.

VINCE: I'm not talking about the police.

JON: So what're you talking about?

VINCE: I dunno. Her.

JON: I think she already knows.

VINCE: Maybe you should apologize.

JON: Oh Jesus—

VINCE: What?

JON: You want me to *apologize* to her?

VINCE: Why not?

JON: It wasn't even date rape, Vince!—It was just something that got a little out of hand—

VINCE: I thought you weren't sure what date rape was.

JON: Look—I'm sorry.

VINCE: Don't apologize to me.

JON: *(Recomposing)* I'm not. What I'm trying to say is that ten years ago I did something wrong, and when I think about it now, it seems like the person who did that is a complete stranger to me. A dumb, drunk, high-school senior who thought she was just being a little prudish and needed some coercion. It was bad and I regret it but it was a far cry from rape. And I don't think *she* would look back on it and call it that either.

VINCE: What *would* she call it?—

JON: I don't know what she'd call it—

VINCE: What if she called it rape?—

JON: Listen to me, I highly, highly doubt that she even remembers it—

VINCE: *You* remember it—

JON: I remember it because it was a pivotal thing for me—

VINCE: Your *first* rape?

JON: Stop being an asshole—

VINCE: Tell me why it was pivotal.

JON: Because it was one of the first times I looked at myself objectively and decided that I would try to avoid becoming a certain type of person. Okay? For her it might have been nothing particularly important one way or another; for me, it constituted something more significant.

VINCE: So you'd like to think.

JON: Why are you suddenly high and mighty?—

VINCE: I'm not high and mighty—I'm too *high* to be high and mighty! I'm just a lowly, drug-dealing, boxer-wearing scum of the earth.

JON: You said it—

VINCE: No, actually, *you* did—

JON: I didn't mean it like that—

VINCE: How'd you mean it?—

JON: That you should change your life a bit—

VINCE: This coming from a rapist—

JON: You're an idiot—

VINCE: Sorry—this coming from a big low-budget moviemaker who makes movies about "where society is possibly headed if we can just manage to forget about that date rape we didn't *kind of* really commit in high school."

JON: You're seriously disturbed.

VINCE: No, actually, I *am* high and mighty. I was wrong before.

JON: What do you want me to say, Vince?—I'm sorry.

VINCE: Stop apologizing to *me*, Jon—

JON: I'm not! I'm apologizing in general. I wish it had never happened. I don't think I'm an evil person.

VINCE: No one's saying you're evil—

JON: It sure as hell feels like it—

VINCE: Do *you* think you're evil?

JON: No—

VINCE: So then you're not evil. *I'm* the evil one here. You're the morally conscious movie-maker.

JON: Whatever—

VINCE: Whatever—

JON: Can we stop now?—

VINCE: Totally—

JON: *Thank you.*

VINCE: *(Beats...)* I just think you should call her.

JON: I'm not gonna call her.

VINCE: I think you should—

JON: Stop! Okay? To call her would be to trivialize the entire matter. It would be like saying, "How's life—oh by the way, sorry I date-raped you ten years ago."

VINCE: So you *did* date-rape her?

JON: No, I didn't—

VINCE: What *did* you do?

JON: I coerced her to have sex with me.

VINCE: How?

JON: Verbally.

VINCE: You verbally coerced her?

JON: Yes. By applying excessive linguistic pressure, I persuaded her to have sex with me.

VINCE: And *then* things got rough?

JON: Things got rough in that after awhile they became aggressively playful.

VINCE: *They* did?

JON: We did.

VINCE: Meaning what?

JON: Meaning I probably still thought I was being playful but others might interpret my actions as being rough.

VINCE: —i.e., rape.

JON: No—rough.

VINCE: Look—Jon, only you two know what happened, so only you two can "interpret" your actions. So why don't you just tell me the facts and interpret them later.

JON: I'm telling you—I argued her into it—

VINCE: You're fucking *lying*, Jon!

(Silence)

JON: What is your problem?

VINCE: How can you sit here with your oldest friend in the world and continuously tell lies?

JON: What makes you think I'm lying?

VINCE: Because only *you* would come up with the term "excessive linguistic pressure". That's not a normal expression, Jon, it's a clear sign of excessive bullshit. If you had really done only that, you'd be more specific. You'd say that you told her that if she didn't put out you'd start telling people she had V D, or smelled bad, or had a penis, or any of the *normal* things that guys say. But *you* come up with your typical crap, which *sounds* mature but contains *nothing!* But it's bullshit, because the reason you are where you are today is because you always insist on getting things your way. It's what you're good at, Jon, so why don't you just own up and admit what you did?!

JON: *(Beat)* Fuck off, Vince. *(He heads for the door.)*

VINCE: Fine. *I'll* call her. *(He reaches for the phone.)*

JON: Don't do that.

VINCE: Why not?—

JON: Because I would like you not to—

VINCE: Why not?—

JON: Because you've already made your point—

VINCE: What's my point?—

JON: Your point is that nobody's perfect, including me, so it offends you when I tell you how I think you should live your life.

VINCE: That's not my point—

JON: It should be—

VINCE: It's not—

JON: Why?—

VINCE: Because I haven't gotten to my point yet—

JON: So then get to it—

VINCE: Maybe I don't have one—

JON: Then I'm gonna go—

VINCE: Wrong—

JON: No—right.

(JON *starts for the door but* VINCE *beats him to it, locks the door, and stands firmly in front of it.*)

VINCE: Admit it.

JON: Admit what?

VINCE: What you did to Amy.

JON: What even makes you think I did something?

VINCE: Because I know—

JON: How?—

VINCE: Because she told me—

JON: Told you what?—

VINCE: What you did—

JON: What did she say?—

VINCE: What?—

JON: What did she say?

VINCE: …Nothing.

JON: Get outta my way, Vincent.

VINCE: It was obvious—

(JON *reaches for the door handle only to have* VINCE *shove him forcefully in the chest. The confrontation has reached a whole new level.*)

VINCE: Tell me what you did and I'll let you go.

JON: Stop being a dick—

VINCE: Tell me what you did—

JON: Why do you care?

VINCE: 'Cause I wanna hear it—

JON: What would that change?

VINCE: I don't know!—

JON: So then what does it matter?—we both know I did something wrong!—

VINCE: So then tell me!—

JON: I pinned her arms back and stuck my dick in! Okay?! For Christ fucking sakes! Shit happens! I already said I'm sorry! *(Silence…)*

VINCE: Thank you.

(VINCE steps away from JON, goes to his duffel bag, reaches inside and carefully rummages around for a second. JON looks on with exhaustion and curiosity. After a moment, VINCE takes out a small tape recorder from the bag. He looks at it briefly to make sure it is still running, then presses the "stop" button. He then places the tape recorder on the floor in front of him. Beat. JON, having registered the import of this, stares at the recorder, and then at VINCE. More silence)

JON: What're you doing?

VINCE: I taped our conversation.

JON: *(Pause)* Why?

VINCE: I wanted to make sure I heard you right.

(Beat; VINCE picks up the recorder, presses "rewind" briefly, then presses "play." Tape: "I pinned her arms back and stuck my dick in! Okay?! For Christ fucking sakes! Shit happens!" He presses "stop." Beat)

VINCE: I guess you're right—you *are* a completely different person.

JON: *(Hollow shock)* I can't believe you just did that.

(VINCE *now takes a sticker label for the tape and writes on it, then methodically places the label onto the tape. He then puts the tape in the pocket of his pants, which lay strewn on the bed. He puts his pants on. He then goes to his bag once more and takes out two beers.*)

VINCE: Beer?

(JON *does not respond, still staring in disbelief at the recorder.* VINCE *tosses the beer anyway. Without looking up,* JON *smacks the beer out of midair, back in the direction of* VINCE. *Pause*)

VINCE: You're mad?

JON: How could you do something like that?

VINCE: Like what?

JON: I'm not messing around, Vince—

VINCE: It offends you?

JON: It offends me fucking immensely.

VINCE: Why?

JON: I'm not even…

VINCE: All I'm suggesting is that you call her up and apologize for the actions of a drunk high-school senior.

JON: *(Pause)* You know you just ended our friendship.

VINCE: It's a cheap little tape recorder. It's Kmart, man.

JON: Why did you do that?

VINCE: I'm trying to make a point.

JON: Which is what?

VINCE: That there's something wrong here.

JON: Where?—With you and me?

VINCE: *(Firm)* Yeah. And everyone else.

JON: You think that everyone else in the world should call up and apologize for what they've done wrong in their life?

VINCE: I don't know.

JON: You honestly think that would *help?* You don't think it'd just end up being a bunch of hypocrites walking around raping people and apologizing?

VINCE: You have a better idea?

JON: *(Firm)* Yeah—not do it next time.

VINCE: That's it?

JON: Yeah.

VINCE: You don't even think she'd want it for herself?

JON: Want *what?*

VINCE: The tape.

JON: Why would she want it?

VINCE: To know that you admitted it.

JON: I doubt she even remembers it happening, Vince.

VINCE: So then she might wanna be reminded.

JON: Why?

VINCE: Because *I'd* wanna be reminded if you pinned down my arms and fucked *me* without permission.

JON: Don't talk like that—

VINCE: That's what you did, Jon, it's on the tape.

JON: This is ridiculous!

VINCE: Why?

JON: Because my apologizing now won't make a difference to her. She's probably dealt with the whole issue and moved on.

VINCE: Maybe she has, but if you're such a different guy than you were ten years ago, then you technically shouldn't have a problem apologizing for something that, in effect, the *real* you didn't even do. Now, on the other hand, if you're still the kind of guy who *could* do something like that, then I can understand your feeling hesitant to apologize. Wouldn't want to come across as a hypocrite.

JON: *(Beat)* Give me the tape.

VINCE: No way.

JON: Why not?

VINCE: Because as you imply to me on a daily basis whenever we spend the day together—I wouldn't have the guts to *tell* her all the interesting tidbits that this tape herewith contains. It'll be much easier to simply *hand* it to her. If I even have the guts to do *that*. *(He goes into his duffel bag again and takes out a tiny plastic bag. He goes to the table and lays out three lines of coke, arranging them carefully with the edge of a credit card taken from his pocket.)* I think I'm gonna skip dinner. I'm not really hungry. *(He snorts a line of coke.)*

JON: You're not gonna give her that tape, Vince.

VINCE: Hard to say.

JON: Tell me what you're gonna do with it.

VINCE: Hard to say. *(He snorts another line of coke.)*

JON: Stop being a dick.

VINCE: I'm sorry—did you want some?

JON: What are you gonna do with the tape?

VINCE: Well…I was *thinking about* making it into a movie and applying to next year's Lansing Film Festival. *(Sits at table calmly)* Seriously, you should go. *(Beat)* I'll tell her you said hello.

JON: What're you talking about?

VINCE: She should be calling any minute.

JON: Why?

VINCE: 'Cause she said she'd call me at eight.

JON: I thought you said you didn't call her.

VINCE: No, I said I *thought* about calling her. And I actually *did*. It's cool. We're hooking up for dinner. *(He sits at the table, placing the tape in front of him. He snorts the last line of coke.)* Really, Jon, you should go. I mean, I probably won't even follow through with the whole thing. *(Beat)* Unless of course, she sees it sitting there and keeps pestering me about what it is.

(Beats. VINCE sips his beer. JON does not know whether to stay or go. Beat. The phone rings. VINCE looks at JON, faux shock...then answers. Sweet as pie:)

VINCE: Hello? ...Hey, Amy! How are you? ...Yeah? Well, are you still up for some chow? ...Cool. By the way, did I even *tell* you why I was out here? ... That's true, the film festival, but the reason for that is because—well you remember Jon Saltzman, right? ... Yeah? Well he's actually made a movie that's being shown as *part* of the festival, so I came out for that... huh? ...Yeah, he *is* out here, staying at the Radisson... hmm-hmm, eleventh floor, overlooking a park. Anyway, so, I don't know how you wanna work this, I'm over at the Motel 6 on Saginaw...exactly... cool, well only thing is that I don't have wheels, so maybe—... well that'd be great, if you wanna just pick me up and we can take it from there...Great, so you know where it is? ...Cool, I'm in room thirty-two... Okay, I'll see you in a few... Bye now. *(He hangs up the phone and begins to get dressed.)* Dude, can I borrow a couple bucks?

JON: Why are you doing this?

VINCE: Well, at first it was a moral crusade, but now I'm not really sure except for the fact that you don't want me to.

JON: And that's worth more than our entire friendship?

VINCE: Jon, if you weren't my oldest friend, I don't think I would have ever assumed that I possess the power to make you think twice about something like this. Assuming you *are* thinking twice.

JON: There are better ways to go about making someone do that.

VINCE: How? Convince you with a really good argument? Apply excessive linguistic pressure? *(No answer)* I'm not a very moral guy, Jon, much less a highly articulate poet-moviemaker. I can barely pay my rent much less persuade someone like *you* to stop being an asshole.

JON: No one's asking you to be articulate, Vince, it's just that you pick potentially the most important weekend of my life to bring up something I haven't even *thought* about in ten years!

VINCE: *(Beat)* Yeah. I guess so. *(He is now full dressed and ready to go.)* You gonna stay here?

JON: Give me the tape.

VINCE: No.

JON: It doesn't belong to you—

VINCE: I *bought* it at Kmart!!!

JON: What's *on* it doesn't belong—

VINCE: Bullshit! I had to be like Aldrich fucking Ames to make this tape. It's the most planned-out thing I've done my whole life!

JON: It's *mine.*, Vince

VINCE: I'm gonna give it to you and you're gonna destroy it.

JON: No I'm not.

VINCE: What're you gonna do?—Put it in your closet and not think about it for *another* ten years?

JON: Where did you get this whole self-righteous thing? It's really not like you to have a spine.

VINCE: What can I say? I'm a fireman.

JON: *(Sitting on bed)* I'm not leaving until you give it up.

VINCE: I don't care if you're not leaving, just don't finish my coke.

JON: Tell me something—have you ever done something that you regretted?

VINCE: Yes—

JON: That you never apologized for?—

VINCE: Yes—

JON: So then why're you doing this now?

VINCE: I don't know! It must be because I have guilt about all that stuff I never apologized for and I'm taking it out on you!

JON: Okay, so then it's irrational.

VINCE: I agree—

JON: So give me the tape—

VINCE: No fucking way! *(Beat)* You know, I wasn't even gonna give it to her at all, but the way you're acting, it's like I have no choice. *(Silence)* She was on her cell, man. Said she was five minutes away.

JON: Give me the tape.

VINCE: No.

JON: Vincent—

VINCE: What?

JON: Give me the tape—

VINCE: Feel free to leave anytime, Jon—

JON: Stop being a dick—

VINCE: —I won't get in your way this time—

JON: VINCENT!

VINCE: *(Mimics)* "VINCENT"!

(Suddenly JON *charges* VINCE *and tackles him onto the bed. Entwined in each other's arms, they now wrestle ferociously, rolling together off the bed and onto the floor. The fight is not so much about the tape as it is about their anger with each other, which is intense, deep-rooted and filled with violent tendencies...although there is also something oddly comic about this wrestling match, seeing as it is the exact type of "roughhousing" they might have done in sixth grade—and yet they are both twenty-eight. It continues, with both alternately gaining an upper edge...until Jon gains an advantage on* VINCE *by pinning him partially up against the base of the wall in a position that looks comfortable for neither man. They remain somewhat stuck here...until there is a knock on the door. They stop struggling. Beats.* VINCE *disengages himself from* JON. *Both boys are now in a state of semi-panic, with Jon looking for possible escape routes, and* VINCE *straightening his hair and tidying the room... After several hurried moments, Jon slips into the bathroom as* VINCE *goes to the door and, still breathing quite heavily, opens it.* AMY RANDALL, *twenty-eight, enters.* VINCE'S *demeanor with* AMY *is like that of a somewhat stoned puppy-dog.)*

VINCE: Hey, Amy—

AMY: Hi, Vincent.

*(*AMY *and* VINCE *give a brief, tentative but genuine hug.)*

VINCE: Wow. You look good.

AMY: You, too—

VINCE: Naw, it's nothing.

(AMY *enters;* JON *haltingly emerges from the bathroom as—*)

VINCE: You're not gonna believe who just showed up—

AMY: …Jon?

JON: Hi, Amy.

AMY: Wow.

JON: Yeah.

AMY: …Quite the reunion—

VINCE: He just swung by to say hello.

AMY: *(To* JON*)* I haven't seen you in…

JON: Since high school, probably.

VINCE: I saw you at Tracy's, right?

AMY: That's right, about five years ago.

JON: I couldn't make it that time.

AMY: That's right. You were in grad school?

JON: U S C.

AMY: For film?—

JON: Yeah.

AMY: Obviously— "Lansing Film Festival"—

JON: Right, that's why I'm here.

AMY: Right. Vince told me.

JON: Right—

AMY: Right. *(Beat…)* I think I'm gonna wait outside, Vincent—

VINCE: No, don't.

AMY: It's just that I didn't lock my car.

VINCE: That's okay. Really. I can watch it from here. *(He looks out the window...)* It's fine. *(He stands next to* AMY, *facing* JON.*)* I'll just stand here.

AMY: O-kay.

(Silence)

VINCE: So.

AMY: Yeah.

(Beat)

VINCE: It's good to see you, Amy.

AMY: You too, Vincent.

VINCE: *(Pause)* So...why do you live in Lansing?

AMY: I guess I like it. It's sort of mellow.

VINCE: Totally.

AMY: I went to school in Ann Arbor.

VINCE: That's right.

AMY: So I just decided to stay.

VINCE: I admire that.

JON: *(Beat)* Vince told me but...what kind of law is it—?

AMY: I'm an assistant district attorney.

JON: Right. That's cool.

AMY: Yeah, I like it a lot.

JON: Yeah?

AMY: Definitely. It's good, it's a pretty good job.

JON: *(Pause)* So you, like, what—you basically... prosecute criminals?

AMY: Yeah.

JON: *(Pause)* Cool.

AMY: Yeah. *(Beat)* So what are *you* up to, Vincent?

VINCE: Me?

AMY: Yeah.

VINCE: Not much.

AMY: I can't believe you just called me out of the blue like that this morning.

VINCE: Yeah?

AMY: I actually love it when people do that.

VINCE: Why?

AMY: I don't know. I never have the courage to do that kind of thing.

VINCE: I just figured what the hell.

AMY: Yeah, but you could've easily *not* done it.

VINCE: Not what?

AMY: Not called. Most people don't.

JON: That's true.

AMY: It *is* true.

VINCE: Like Jon.

JON: *(In explanation)* I didn't know you lived out here.

AMY: And if you had?

JON: I'm probably one of those people who don't have the courage.

AMY: You think?

JON: It's hard to say.

AMY: It is. Half the time it's not even worth it. People change…

VINCE: *(Beat)* I'm glad you're not fat.

AMY: Is that right?

VINCE: Yeah.

AMY: You should of seen me in college.

VINCE: Fat?

AMY: Quite.

VINCE: Me too.

AMY: Probably for different reasons. *(Beat...)* So, you didn't answer my question.

VINCE: Which one?

AMY: What are you doing these days?

VINCE: Oh. I live in California.

AMY: Where?

VINCE: Oakland.

AMY: ...Nice.

VINCE: I'm a firefighter.

AMY: Are you serious?

VINCE: I'm totally serious.

AMY: That's pretty cool, Vincent.

VINCE: It keeps me busy.

AMY: I'm sure.

VINCE: Yeah.

AMY: *(Beat)* Lotta fires in Oakland?

VINCE: Average.

JON: I should get going.

VINCE: I thought you were coming to dinner with us.

JON: No, I never said that.

VINCE: Well why don't you?

JON: I can't, I gotta get some sleep for tomorrow.

VINCE: No you don't—

JON: Yeah, actually, I do—

VINCE: Dude, they're showing your *movie,* you're not running a marathon—

JON: I know, but—

VINCE: Plus they're showing it at two o'clock in the afternoon.

JON: I know, but I have some meetings in the morning.

AMY: You haven't changed, have you, Vincent?

VINCE: Whattayou mean?

AMY: I can remember you doing the exact same thing when we were dating.

VINCE: Doing what?

AMY: Putting pressure on people to follow your schedule.

VINCE: That's not true.

AMY: It *is,* but it's nice. It's like you stayed up the night before thinking for hours how the next day was going to work and now you just want people to partake in your vision.

VINCE: Okay, Amy, that's not true—

AMY: Okay—

VINCE: Jon can do anything he wants—

AMY: I know—

VINCE: I'm just suggesting he joins us for dinner.

JON: Why?

VINCE: Because I'm sentimental. Is that so wrong? I like it when old friends get together. It makes me feel warm.

AMY: Maybe Jon doesn't feel like it—

VINCE: I know he doesn't because he doesn't have the courage. It's like you said, he lets these things go.

AMY: I didn't mean him specifically.

VINCE: Well you should have. He always does it.

JON: Does what?

VINCE: Lets things go. If you saw your mother on the street, you'd cross to the other side.

JON: What are you—high?

VINCE: Yes.

AMY: *(Pause)* Are you high, Vincent?

VINCE: …A bit.

AMY: You've been smoking pot since high school?

VINCE: It's no different than drinking—

AMY: I know, but do you also still drink?—

VINCE: So?

AMY: I'm just saying you should be careful—

VINCE: What is this, "Lecture Vince Night"?

AMY: Who's lecturing you?

VINCE: *You* are. *He* did, I'm waiting for the Motel 6 *desk* guy to come in here next.

AMY: It's only because I care about you.

VINCE: You haven't seen me for five years.

AMY: But you were my first boyfriend. It's inevitable. You could turn into a dirty old man and I'd still care.

VINCE: Really?

AMY: Of course. It's one of those things.

VINCE: *(Beat)* Do you wanna get married?

AMY: I can't right now.

VINCE: Why?

AMY: I have a boyfriend.

VINCE: Who is he?

AMY: He's the district attorney.

VINCE: That is so typical!…

AMY: Why?

VINCE: I don't know, it just is …

AMY: If it doesn't work out, I'll give you a call in Oakland.

VINCE: Yeah, right—

JON: So I should get going.

VINCE: *(To* AMY*)* Why don't you give *him* a lecture?

AMY: On what?

VINCE: Taking better care of himself.

AMY: He looks like he's doing okay.

JON: *(Standing.)* It was good to see you again, Amy.

VINCE: Whoa, whoa, whoa—

AMY: Vince—

VINCE: No, he's not getting out of here just like that.

JON: Maybe I'll see you tomorrow.

VINCE: No, bullshit!—

JON: Vince—

VINCE: What?!

JON: I have to go. *(Beat; he reaches out to shake* AMY*'s hand.)*

VINCE: You see, it's actually really nice of you to say that, Amy, because I always thought *Jon* was your first love. *(Beat)* I mean, I know you guys didn't really date that much, but I guess I always assumed—even though I didn't know about it 'til later—I always assumed that when you guys got together there at the end of senior year, it was sort of like some long-awaited love affair that was bound to happen. *(Beat)* Am I characterizing that correctly?

JON: *(Beat)* I don't think anyone would call it a long-awaited love affair, Vince.

VINCE: What would you call it?

JON: I'd call it us getting together at the end of senior year.

VINCE: *(Pause; to* AMY*)* Oh. Maybe I'm just jealous because…you know, *I* wanted to be your first boyfriend.

AMY: You were.

VINCE: I know, but…you know what I mean.

AMY: Oh.

VINCE: I shouldn't care about that kind of stuff, but like I say, I'm sentimental.

AMY: That's not sentimental, Vincent.

VINCE: What is it?

AMY: It's stupid.

VINCE: …I agree, but see, I didn't know that in high school. Back then, you not wanting to have sex with me was sort of like being disinvited to Christmas dinner at my grandparents. *(Pause)* Which is something I'm very sentimental about.

AMY: You shouldn't have taken it personally.

VINCE: I know, but I did. *(Pause)* Especially when you guys ended up getting together. Literally. *(Quietly to* AMY*)* But I guess I blew it out of proportion.

AMY: What're you talking about?

VINCE: I'm talking about you guys getting together at the end of senior year. It hurt my feelings at the time. But according to Jon, it was less of a long-awaited love affair and more like just two kids getting giddy before graduation. In which case, I suppose I really shouldn't hold a grudge. *(Beat)* Is that what it was?

AMY: *(Beat)* I would say that it was a crush that never amounted to much.

VINCE: For you or for him?

AMY: For me.

JON: Vince, it doesn't seem like Amy really wants to talk about this.

VINCE: Why not, we're all mature adults. We can talk about a high-school crush that happened ten years ago.

JON: Fine, then I'm gonna let you two have this discussion without me.

VINCE: Okay, but before you leave, I'm just curious as to why nothing ever came of Amy's crush for you. Amy?

AMY: Why nothing ever came of it?

VINCE: Yeah. Why *didn't* it develop into something more serious. I mean, it wasn't like you and I got back together afterwards. I don't think you even dated anyone after that. At least not anybody from our school.

AMY: *(Beat)* I guess it just didn't work out.

VINCE: Oh. *(Pause. Gentle:)* And there's no specific reason for that?

AMY: I'm sure there was.

VINCE: But?

AMY: No but. I'm sure there was.

VINCE: Oh. *(Beat)* Why're you so anxious to leave, Jon?

JON: Because this is awkward for me.

VINCE: And so you'd rather *leave?*

JON: Fine, Vince. *(He stretches his arms out, palms up.)* Here I am. Would anyone like to say anything to me? *(Silence)* Amy?

AMY: *(Beat…)* No thanks.

JON: Vince?

VINCE: Yeah.

(VINCE takes the tape from his pocket and tosses it to JON.)

VINCE: It's your call, Jon. I can't speak for you.

(JON holds the tape; silence.)

JON: *(Beat…)* It was good to see you again, Amy.

AMY: *(Pause)* You too.

VINCE: *(To self)* That is so fucking typical…

JON: I gotta go.

(JON prepares to leave, with a small, unsuccessful attempt to make eye contact with AMY before doing so… He opens the door—)

VINCE: Jon?

JON: What?

VINCE: Can I have that back?

(Beat)

JON: Okay.

(JON tosses VINCE the tape; beat.)

JON: Goodbye, Amy.

(AMY does not answer. Beat; JON exits. Silence…)

AMY: Oakland must be a pretty safe place.

VINCE: Why?

AMY: There don't seem to be enough fires to keep you busy.

VINCE: What do you mean?

AMY: Can you tell me what that was about?

VINCE: I wanted to know what happened between you two.

AMY: When?

VINCE: That night. *(Beat)* I wanted him to apologize to you.

AMY: Why?

VINCE: So you could hear it. *(Beat)* He admitted it to me.

AMY: What did you do?

VINCE: I got him to admit it. It's on the tape.

AMY: Admit what?

VINCE: What he did to you.

(No answer)

VINCE: He did do it, didn't he? Amy? *(Beat)* That night. Am I wrong? *(Beat. Gentle:)* He raped you. Didn't he?

AMY: *(Pause)* Why would that be any of your business?

VINCE: You're missing my point—

AMY: And even if he had, the last thing I would want is a taped confession.

VINCE: Why not?

AMY: Because I'm not the one who needs it.

VINCE: What're you talking about?

*(*AMY *starts to leave.)*

AMY: I'm not the one who needs it.

VINCE: So then who needs it?

AMY: I'll see you later—

VINCE: Where are you going?

AMY: Home.

VINCE: I don't think you understand, I was trying to do the right thing.

AMY: *(Turning back to him)* For whom?

VINCE: For you.

AMY: Is that really what you mean, Vincent?

VINCE: I thought you'd appreciate it.

AMY: Well I don't.

VINCE: Why not?

AMY: Because he didn't rape me. *(Beats.)*

VINCE: What? *(Pause)*

AMY: He didn't. *(Pause)* So the only person you're trying to make feel better is yourself.

(Silence. Beat. Then a knock on the door. Beat. VINCE puts the tape back in his pocket. He goes and opens the door. JON is there. He looks at them both; beat.)

JON: Hey.

VINCE: *(Pause)* Hey.

(JON closes the door behind him and enters the room more fully; more silence.)

VINCE: What are you doing?

JON: I came back.

VINCE: Why?

JON: Because I felt like it. *(Beat)* Vince, can you give us a couple minutes in private?

VINCE: *(Beat)* Are you kidding me?

JON: I'm serious.

VINCE: You want me to leave you alone with her?

JON: Yeah—

VINCE: No—

JON: You can wait outside the door.

VINCE: No fucking way!

JON: Why not?

VINCE: Because of the whole—no. No.

JON: I just need two minutes—

VINCE: Why?

JON: I want to tell her something.

VINCE: What?

JON: It's none of your business.

VINCE: Yes it is—

JON: Why?

VINCE: Because I'm the one who brought it up!

AMY: It's all right, Vincent.

VINCE: No it's not.

AMY: Yes it is.

VINCE: Well I don't care, I'm not leaving!

(VINCE *folds his arms and sits down. Silence. Beat;* JON *turns to* AMY.)

JON: I wanted to apologize.

VINCE: For what?

JON: Vince—

VINCE: What?!

JON: Shut up! *(Beat; to* AMY, *genuine.)* I wanted to apologize. *(Beat)* For what it's worth. *(Pause)* I'm sorry. I really, honestly, truly am.

(Silence...)

AMY: For what?

JON: For what happened between us in high school.

AMY: What happened between us?

JON: I'm talking about what happened at the end of senior year, which Vince was trying to get me to talk about before.

AMY: Before when?

JON: Like five minutes ago.

AMY: About when you and I got together in high school?

JON: Right.

AMY: Right. So tell me again what happened?

JON: (Beat) Do you know which day I'm talking about?

AMY: At the end of senior year? At Rebecca's party?

JON: Yeah.

AMY: Yeah.

VINCE: (Beat) What are you guys doing?

AMY: I'm just curious. I don't want there to be a communication gap here.

JON: I'm not sure what I'm supposed to say.

AMY: I think you think you did something to me.

JON: Yes.

AMY: What do you think you did?

JON: Why?

AMY: Because this is very interesting to me.

JON: Do you not think something happened?

AMY: Well of course something happened.

JON: But are you saying you don't remember what it was?

AMY: C'mon, Jon—there are certain things one doesn't forget.

JON: I agree.

AMY: I'm just wondering how you would describe it.

JON: Probably the same way as you.

AMY: You think?

JON: *(Beat)* The whole reason this thing started is because Vince taped this conversation he and I had earlier.

VINCE: Dude, I'm sorry—

JON: It's fine—

VINCE: I didn't realize—

JON: I'm just saying, that that's why I'm here.

AMY: You're here because Vince taped you?

JON: Yes.

AMY: Why?

JON: *Why?*

AMY: Why?

JON: ...Because it made me think.

AMY: Oh.

JON: Which is why I came back.

AMY: Good—so tell me what happened.

JON: *(Beat...)* I think I raped you.

AMY: *(Beat...)* No. You didn't rape me.

JON: *(Beat)* Yes I did.

AMY: No. You didn't.

JON: *(Beat)* Are you trying to make fun of this?

AMY: No.

JON: Amy. I *know* what happened.

AMY: Says who?

JON: Me.

AMY: Why?

JON: Because I just admitted it.

AMY: On what—the tape?

JON: Yeah.

AMY: What's on it?

JON: It's me confessing what I did.

AMY: But that doesn't prove you *did* it—

JON: Why not?—

AMY: Because if no one's accusing you of anything, then there's no reason to confess.

JON: ...I'm having trouble realizing what you're doing.

AMY: I'm not doing anything—

JON: This is not an easy thing for me.

AMY: You sure about that?

VINCE: Jon?

JON: What?

VINCE: Do you know what you're saying?

JON: I'm saying what you wanted me to say.

VINCE: But are you sure you have the right girl?

JON: Yes!

VINCE: She says nothing happened.

JON: She's lying—

AMY: No I'm not.

JON: Amy, you're mocking this!

AMY: Why would I do that?

JON: I don't know, but if you are, I have better things to do.

AMY: I just think we just have differing perceptions of what happened.

JON: I really don't see how that could be.

AMY: Why, because *you* decided you did something?

JON: I *did* do something.

AMY: Well I say you didn't.

JON: So then what happened?

AMY: We had sex.

JON: Amy, I'm trying to be honest.

AMY: Why now?

JON: Because I haven't *seen* you in ten years.

AMY: But why *now?*

JON: Because when Vince played me back that tape, it hit me what I had done.

AMY: And if he *hadn't* played back the tape?

JON: Yeah—?

AMY: Would you be saying this?

JON: Probably not.

AMY: Or is it just that I'm here?

JON: What do you mean?

AMY: If I lived in Alaska, would you have sought me out?

JON: I don't really know.

AMY: You should look into that.

JON: Fine.

AMY: Or is it that you're jealous.

JON: Of what?

AMY: Vincent and I.

JON: That's ridiculous—

AMY: Why? *I* loved *you.* *(Beat)* I did. I was totally in love with you that night. *(Beat...)* Did you love me?

JON: *(Beat)* No.

AMY: So why were you with me?

JON: I'm not sure.

AMY: Maybe it's the same reason you came back to apologize just now.

JON: Which is what?

AMY: You like pissing off Vincent.

JON: Why would it piss him off if that's what he wanted in the first place!?

AMY: Because he's confused.

VINCE: Exactly.

AMY: It's never too late to one-up your best friend by telling him once and for all that you raped the love of his life in high school. *(Pause)* Especially if you get to do it in front of her.

JON: You really think I'm like that?

AMY: I don't know, I have a very poor record of judging you accurately. *(Beat)* Maybe you just came back to get the last word. You didn't like what was on the tape, so you came back to hear yourself phrase it more eloquently.

JON: *(Beat)* The reason I came back is to apologize, which I can assure you is not at all disingenuous. I honestly am sorry.

AMY: Why, because you had your hand over my mouth?

JON: *(Pause)* Yes.

AMY: Well hey, Jon...I let everybody do that.

*(Beats…*JON *starts for the door.)*

VINCE: Where are you going?

JON: I think I should leave.

VINCE: Why?—

JON: Because no matter what I say, there's nowhere for this to go.

AMY: *(Strong)* You want the last word, Jon, but it's not yours to have.

VINCE: Why don't you guys just figure out what the fuck you're talking about?!—

JON: Vince!

VINCE: What?

JON: She's in denial.

VINCE: Amy?

AMY: *(To* VINCE*)* What was it that even made you think something happened?

VINCE: At Rebecca's?

AMY: Yeah.

VINCE: Because I thought it did. I thought later that that's what you were trying to tell me.

AMY: Why?

VINCE: Because why else would you have slept with Jon when you were supposed to be dating me?

AMY: You and I had already broken up.

VINCE: I know, but we hadn't even slept together, so what the hell were you doing sleeping with him?

AMY: It's none of your business.

VINCE: Well that's partly why I figured something happened.

AMY: Why, because if I wasn't sleeping with you, why would I sleep with somebody else?

VINCE: Yeah...I guess...I guess...I thought something like that. *(Beat...)*

JON: I'm gonna go. *(To* VINCE*)* Maybe I'll see you tomorrow. Amy, I'm sorry. And I'm sorry you're not in a place where you can hear that right now. *(Pause)* I hope you take good care of yourself. *(He heads for the door.)*

AMY: Why did you say that?

JON: What?

AMY: That I'm not in a place to hear that.

JON: Because you don't seem to realize that I'm serious. I don't know how else to put it to you other than to say what I've said. Even if you really do think it wasn't a big deal, it was for me, and I want you to know that I'm sorry it happened.

*(*JON *finishes, his words lingering in the air a moment. He has made* AMY *think. It seems as though she will not answer him.)*

AMY: *(Beat; calm on the surface.)* Well you *should* be. And I hope you die for it and go to hell; and if there is no hell, I hope that you suffer on your way *to* death, and that your last living sensation is that of a steel rod being shoved repeatedly up your insides so that it batters your heart and punctures your stomach; and when you die and your sphincter finally collapses, my hope is that your last bowel movement be saturated with blood from the draining backwash of your rotted, fucking, pathetic guts! *(Long silence as she "recovers."* To VINCE, *calm.)* Is that along the lines of what you wanted? *(No answer; beat...to* JON*)* I really don't know what you want me to say to you.

JON: *(Pause)* Nothing.

(*Beat.* AMY *has pulled a cell phone from her purse and now calmly dials three numbers…*)

AMY: (*Into her phone.*) Hi, this is Amy Randall from the D A's office, could you please dispatch a squad car over to the Motel 6 on Saginaw, room thirty-two. There seems to be a significant amount of illegal substance in the room…it appears to be cocaine…yes, and also, you might want to run a check on one of the two gentlemen here, Jon Saltzman S-a-l-t-z-m-a-n—possible history of sexual misconduct including a verified first degree C S C ten years prior…thank you.

(AMY *ends the call and returns the phone to her purse. Silence.* JON *and* VINCE *are both staring at her. Beat*)

AMY: You guys can make a run for it if you like.

VINCE: Did you really just do that?

AMY: The average response time in Lansing is four minutes. It's one of the top departments in the country.

JON: Why does it have to be like this?

AMY: Because if you're truly repentant, then you should be willing to pay the price.

JON: Why can't you just accept the fact that I'm sorry?

AMY: It does me no good.

JON: Is that *my* fault?

AMY: No, that's just the way it is.

JON: But *I'm* the one who has to run out of here like a criminal?

AMY: It's up to you.

JON: Because I'm not going to.

AMY: Is that because you think the statute of limitations ran out?

JON: I have no idea.

AMY: There is none for a sexual misconduct felony. *(Pause)* Just to let you know.

VINCE: *(Beat)* Okay—I really don't feel like getting busted for a couple lines of coke.

AMY: Then I guess I'll see you later, Vincent.

(VINCE is unsure what to do for a moment, then he quickly wipes the rest of the cocaine back into the bag and sticks it in his pocket.)

AMY: Just do me a favor and leave that tape behind. *(Pause)* So I can give it to Officer Friendly.

(Pause; VINCE is quite unsure what to do.)

VINCE: You want me to give you the tape?

AMY: Yeah.

(VINCE looks at JON.)

AMY: You don't need his permission.

VINCE: I feel like I do.

AMY: You didn't need his permission to *make* it; why would you need it now?

VINCE: *(Pause)* Protocol?

AMY: Fine, then I'll just stay here and tell them myself.

(VINCE starts to gather up his things.)

VINCE: Dude, it might be in your best interest to come with me.

JON: I'm staying.

VINCE: Why?!

JON: Because maybe she's right: Maybe I should be willing to pay the price.

VINCE: Fine but what about me?!

JON: What *about* you?

VINCE: *I* didn't really do anything wrong!

AMY: You're in possession of illegal substance—

VINCE: I know but I was just trying to blow off some steam.

AMY: You should've blown it off with beer.

VINCE: I *did*, I just needed to blow off a little extra.

JON: You better go, Vince, they're on their way.

VINCE: Come with me.

JON: No.

VINCE: Don't be an idiot, they'll arrest you!!

(JON *remains still. To* AMY)

VINCE: Is this really what you want?

AMY: Jon's a big boy, he can make his own decisions.

VINCE: Fine, then I'm outta here.

JON: Thanks, Vince.

VINCE: What?

JON: Thanks—

VINCE: For what?

JON: For all your honesty.

VINCE: *(At a loss.)* What do you mean?

JON: Nothing. I'll see you later.

(VINCE *starts again for the door, but then stops. He knows he wouldn't be able to live with himself if he left—for it is he who got* JON *into this.)*

VINCE: FUCK!

(*In a change of plans,* VINCE *now hurriedly takes the bag of coke from his pocket, then reaches into his duffel bag and produces an absolutely enormous bag of marijuana; he then takes both bags and goes into the bathroom. We hear the flush of a toilet. A moment later, he comes back out empty-handed; he goes to the table and attempts to wipe clean any*

potential remnants of the cocaine. All of this is done with a
large amount of frustration, sadness, and bitter dejection. He
then goes to the window and looks out. Seeing that he still
has at least a minute or two, he takes the cassette from his
pocket, looks momentarily at JON, *then methodically breaks*
the cassette in half, pulling out the tape so as to ensure
the cassette's total destruction. Finally, he sits on the bed.
Silence. There is silence for quite awhile as the three of them
sit, some perhaps looking at others. Then, a notion slowly
begins to enter VINCE's *mind. Beat...)*

([Option: VINCE *does NOT break the tape before* AMY
leaves, but rather VINCE *takes it out after* AMY *exits and*
it is included as part of the final blackout image of JON *and*
VINCE *at the end of the play. If he has used an I-phone, the*
possibilities are even more plentiful.])

VINCE: Did you really call the police?

AMY: No.

VINCE: *Jesus Christ!!!*

AMY: Sorry.

VINCE: *Why'd you do that?!!*

AMY: I felt like it.

VINCE: YOU ARE SO *FUCKED* UP!!!

AMY: What did you expect?

VINCE: Fine, but do you know how much those drugs
cost?!!

AMY: There'll be other drugs, Vincent.

VINCE: I know, but I really liked *those* ones.

*(Silence...*AMY *now stands; she regards* JON *for a very long*
moment.)

AMY: *(Beat, to* JON) Good luck tomorrow.

JON: Thank you.

AMY: Goodbye, Vincent.

VINCE: Bye, Amy.

(AMY *opens the door to go.*)

VINCE: It was good to see—

(*—but the door is already shut and* AMY *is gone. Beats.* JON *and* VINCE *sit in silence.* VINCE *starts to say something, then decides not to. Beats… Lights fade to black.*)

END OF PLAY

OPTIONAL PROLOGUE

(*A darkened room, lit mainly by the glow of a television set. The voices of two young men can be heard from beyond an open doorway, through which smoke intermittently emanates. Party music can be heard from the other room. [Or: The entire prologue could be seen on a large video projected onto the back wall.]*)

VINCE: Why—for fuck's sake?!!

JON: Maybe she just needed to move on.

VINCE: But we were in love!

JON: Wait—save it for the video.

VINCE: Is it working?

JON: Almost.

VINCE: Did you put the thing in the thing?

JON: What?

VINCE: Put the red thing in the red thing!

JON: That's what she said last night.

VINCE: Dude, that is so fucking stupid. It's like a third-grader.

JON: That's what she said last night.

VINCE: I'm switching to the bong.

JON: Vince?

VINCE: What?

JON: If I'm a banker, in like twenty years—?

VINCE: Yeah?

JON: I want you to come and find me, and kill me.

VINCE: You don't like bankers?

JON: It's what everybody expects.

VINCE: *I* expect you to be a dickwad in twenty years.

JON: Well if I'm a dickwad, then it probably means I'm also a banker.

VINCE: Why—all bankers are dickwads?

JON: You're not listening—

VINCE: I'm totally listening and I frankly find it offensive to bankers!

JON: Whatever. *(Sound of a bong)*

VINCE: Why do you fucking *have* a video camera anyway?

JON: Because I'm chronicling things.

VINCE: Chronicling what?

JON: Things!! We're graduating in two weeks—this is the last time we are who we are.

VINCE: Dude—smoke this.

JON: Hang on—

VINCE: *SMOKE IT!!*

JON: I think it's working.

(The light from the T V reflects moving images.)

VINCE: Hey, I look like Ralph Macchio!

JON: *(Narrates)* Okay—archive, Rebecca's parrty, May 18, senior year in high school: Whattayou got to say, Vince?

VINCE: If I'm a banker in twenty years, I want you to find me and give me a mam-*moth* frickin' bong hit!!!!

JON: *(Still narrating.)* There you have it: folks: The goals and dreams of our next generation.

VINCE: Fuck—

JON: What?

VINCE: Amy's here.

JON: Vince—you gotta get over it.

VINCE: But she looks hot.

JON: She *is* hot.

VINCE: So—?

JON: So that's it. Two weeks from now, it's a whole-new-fucking-ball game!!

END OF OPTIONAL PROLOGUE

OPTIONAL EPILOGUE

(Lights rise on VINCE, *now dressed in casual Eddie Bauer wear, sound of a phone ringing, followed by a machine picking up.)*

JON: *(Voice-over.)* It's Jon, you know what to do. *(Sound of a beep.)*

VINCE: Hey, John. Vince here. *(Pause)* How are you, man? It's been a long time. *(Pause)* I actually tried calling you a few weeks ago, but…your machine said you were on location…in Antarctica, or somewhere, so…I didn't leave a message.
Anyway, I've been thinking about you, I guess. *(Beat)* You'll be happy to know that I finally woke up, after far too many years of not really waking up at all, waking and baking, waking and faking…flaking. I quit the bullshit in Oakland, moved home for awhile, and then about a year ago, I moved up here. To Lansing. *(Beat)* Which probably strikes you as funny, considering everything, but you know what? —It makes sense. *(Pause)* There's some really fine dining out here. *(A small smile; beat)* Anyway, I'm working as a high-school math teacher. I'm also assistant J.V. head football coach. We got robbed last week, fucking Upper Peninsula refs… Anyway, I'm living a pretty quiet life. It's good.
(Beat; deep breath.) I guess the reason I wanted to check in is because about a month ago…I gave Amy a call.

(Beat) We met at a T G I Friday's. I ordered a Diet Coke,
she had a glass of merlot. And we talked. *(Pause)* And I
apologized. For what happened five years ago…in the
motel room. *(Pause)* And she didn't accept. Which was
good. And which I'd expected. *(Beat)*

I've been in love with her for seventeen years, Jon. I
have. And just because it started in high school, does
that make it wrong? If a person strips away everything
about them that's stupid…down to where only the
fundamental feelings are left…and those feelings are
the same as they were when they first met, then aren't
they legitimate? *(Pause)* And I know that change is…
it's a long-term thing…but my question to myself—
and maybe to you—is: If enough of it has occurred
in a person, can't they try again? *(Beat)* I don't think
about her every day. I date other women, I like my
job. *(Pause)* But I have hope. *(Pause)* And maybe one of
these days I'll try again. *(Beat)*

I'm not sure why I'm telling you all this. You're
probably busy, I just…I guess I just wanted to…let you
know. *(Pause)* I hope Antarctica treated you well and
that you didn't…lose your penis to frostbite. *(Pause)*
Let's talk soon. Love you.

(Beat…)

OPERATOR. *(Voice-over)* If you'd like to make a call,
please hang up and try your call again; if you'd like to
make a call, please hang up and try your call again.

*(Loud noise which accompanies that message…as lights
cross-fade to* JON, *who sits in a large armchair speaking to
us tight-shot on camera, through a projected, highly defined
digital video image.)*

JON: Archive, April third. *(Beat)* This is gonna sound
completely off the wall but I'm just gonna say it: I've
been thinking about becoming a Unitarian minister.
That's what I've been thinking about. *(Beat)*

Unitarianism is an incredibly profound religion,
to a great extent, I believe, because of its use of
intuition. And keep in mind that we're in a day and
age when no one really intuits anymore. We do
just about everything *but* intuit. We insist, demand,
deduce, ascertain, "base on faith," kill Everything but
intuit. Except for the Unitarians. These people intuit
everything, not the least of which is God. They find
God manifested in a grain of sand; in the glint of a
lizard's eye. And I have to say that appeals to me.
Because frankly I'm tired. I'm tired of…using plastic
silverware and talking about yoga. *(Pause)* I really just
wanna live a more honest life.
(Beat) I found these tapes the other day. Mostly stupid
shit, me interviewing friends, blabbering about the end
of high school. *(Pause)* And I thought of Vince. *(Beat)*
I literally haven't seen the guy in ten years. Since that
night in the motel room. We've talked, e-mailed, done
all the peripheral shit. But we haven't seen each other.
(Beat) So I called him. Up there in Michigan. And I said,
"Hey Vince, what're you doing?" And he said, "I'm
raising my kid." And I said, "How is it?" And he said,
"It's great, Jon, it really, truly is."
And when I hung up, I thought about the last time I
saw him. And I thought, "Jesus Christ we've changed.
Vince has a kid, he's not a drunk, he's…happy." And
then, inevitably—maybe because I'm a filmmaker,
or because I'm a shitty Hollywood filmmaker—I
inevitably looked in the mirror, and I asked myself if
I'd changed. Over ten years. Over twenty. *(Pause)* And
to tell you the truth, I wasn't sure what the answer
was. *(He now points a remote control device in the direction
of the camera and zooms very close-up on his still-youthful
face; pause; very honest.)*
I've thought about nothing over the last ten years
except for what happened that night. Nothing. I've

made six movies, I've bought a house with a fucking swing that swings out over the Pacific, and I've been married and divorced and occasionally in love, but I have thought about nothing except that night. *(Beat)* And maybe that sounds like bullshit, unless you know the kinds of thought I'm talking about, the late-night kinds when you're driving near cliffs, when you're banging a twenty-two-year-old, when you're staring at the wall with a bottle of Aleve in your fucking hand. *(Beat)* And if you asked me what I've thought about exactly, all those years—I wouldn't have a clue what to answer. It's not guilt, it's not my lost friendship with Vince, it's not even Amy so much, if truth be told. *(Pause)* I've just thought. *(Beat)* About who I am. Who I'm not. Who I would like to be capable of being. *(Beat)* And the thing, or perhaps I should say, the only thing that I've come up with after ten years…is that I think I wanna be a Unitarian minister. *(Beat)*
I'm thirty-eight years old. *(Pause)* I have a lot of time left.

(JON now points a remote control device in the direction of the camera…and turns himself off. He then presses another button and…a moment later, AMY's grainy image appears on a dated, handheld camcorder; she's dressed a bit like an early Madonna.)

JON: *(Voice-over)* Archive, Rebecca's party, May eighteenth—

AMY: What are you doing?

JON: *(Voice-over)* It's like a chronicle…about…whatever, the end of school. Like…like what do you think everything's gonna be like after graduation?

AMY: I dunno. I mean, I'll definitely miss things.

JON: *(Voice-over)* Like Vince?

AMY: No. *(Pause)* I mean, yeah, but…*you* saw him just now—he gets pissed, slams the door and now he'll drive around drunk all night listening to like, *Yaz,* or whatever. *(Pause)* You're not gonna show him this, are you?

JON: *(Voice-over)* No.

AMY: I dunno…I keep having this dream where after graduation I take everything I've done for the last four years and put it in, like, a crystal box…and blow the whole thing to fucking smithereens. And just walk away forever. *(Beat)*
But then sometimes in the dream I *keep* the box—instead of blowing it away—so that whenever I'm lost or fucked up, I can retrace my steps back and crawl inside and say, "Yeah, this is where I came from. This is who I am."
I dunno. I guess *neither* of those are…*realistic.* 'Cause you can't really *destroy* your past, and you also can't crawl back inside it. *(Pause)* Maybe the best we can do is sort of…drag the box along behind us…and occasionally look inside…and appreciate its beauty. *(Beat; she looks at the camera, then smiles embarrassingly… and perhaps flirtatiously…)* What? …What?

END OF OPTIONAL EPILOGUE

THE TRANSPARENCY OF VAL

THE TRANSPARENCY OF VAL was first produced by Trustus Theater (Jim Thigpen, Artistic Director) in Columbia South Carolina, opening on 5 August 2000. The cast and creative contributors were:

VAL .... Alex Smith
ACTOR #1 .... Anne Kelly
ACTOR #2 .... S Jack Silman
ACTOR #3 .... Thomas Edward Dalton
ACTOR #4 .... Jonathan Whitton
ACTOR #5 .... Darion McCloud
ACTOR #6 .... Marilyn Matheus

Director & Set design .... Jayce Tromsness
Lighting design .... Robert Carter
Sound design .... Dorothea Reiger
Production stage manager .... Charlie Harrell

THE TRANSPARENCY OF VAL was first produced in New York by Captains of Industry in association with Theater Outrageous and Elizabeth Timperman at Clemente Soto-Velez Cultural Center, opening on 18 July 2002. The cast and creative contributors were:

VAL	Jonathan Green
ACTOR #1	Veronica Goode
ACTOR #2	George Hannah
ACTOR #3	Karl Herlinger
ACTOR #4	Joan Jubet
ACTOR #5	Mike Timony
ACTOR #6	Pamela Hart
Director	Sam Helfrich
Set design	David Newell
Lighting design	Thom Weaver
Costume design	Jennifer Halpern
Production stage manager	Jana Llynn

CHARACTERS & SETTING

VAL, *a young man, to be played by either a white, Latino or mixed race actor.*

Actor #1, Black female, 30ish. To play parts of RITA, DR BYSMA

Actor #2, White male, 40ish, to play parts of SAL, DRAFT OFFICER, OLD MAN, MAN

Actor #3, White male, 40ish, to play parts of MR RHEUM, PROF SEBUM, RICH, BARTENDER, WINSTON, GOVERNMENT OFFICIAL, PRISON GUARD, PURE

Actor #4, Female, male or trans, 27ish, to play part of RUDI, DOLLY PARTON, CHAPLAIN

Actor #5, Black male, 27ish, to play parts of NEW, BILLY, RON, OLD WINDOW WASHER, KIRBY, JAKE

Actor #6, Female of any race (preferably non-anglo), 27ish, to play parts of PRO, WILLA, MOTHER TERESA, KARA

The sets and costumes for this play are numerous and should be rendered with ease and simplicity. There is no need for them to be particularly extensive, naturalistic or complex in their design)

Note: The "camp" potential in this play should be generally played against, *meaning a grounded, quite simplistic approach to often illogical and hopefully comic scenes should be taken. For example, the breastfeeding in Scene 1 should be*

shown to be the simple, quite normal act that it is, despite the fact an adult character is actually doing the suckling. While it can be fun, it should not be silly.

Optional live drums are suggested throughout the piece.

Casting note: although the specific casting requirements listed below are encouraged, a director is welcome to alter them according to the angle of emphasis he or she decides to take on the play. Be advised, however, that each choice invariably effects the others in intense and "loaded" ways. Please consider the entirety of the piece if and when straying from the preceding suggestions.

AUTHOR'S NOTE

The Howard Zinn collection, *The Zinn Reader,* was very helpful in locating certain facts for this play.

Scene 1

(RITA *and* SAL *sit in their house, a conservative, pretty dwelling. She nurses their newborn son. She is loving, He is gruff, but with a tender heart buried beneath. To the side stands* VAL, *naked, facing out. He is the grown-up version of their son. A second option is that he is, in fact, suckling from his mother's breast.*)

RITA: He's breathing, Sal.

SAL: That's how it works.

RITA: It's nice.

SAL: Yes.

RITA: I can feel each breath. Like for the first time.

SAL: Yes.

RITA: (*Beat*) I love you.

SAL: I love you too. (*He is silent, watching out over the distance.*)

RITA: Will we teach him that? To love. To have faith in love, instead of hate.

SAL: We'll teach him everything we know. "Train up a child in the way he should go and when he is old he will not depart from it."

RITA: And the mistakes we will make?

SAL: They will be laced with wisdom, a silver lining of knowledge embedded in a golden platter.

RITA: A platter of our mistakes…

SAL: Piled high with our shortcomings, adorned with our wisdom, garnished with our hope.

RITA: And then he shall go forth unto the world......

SAL: And he will become.

RITA: What will he become, Sal?

SAL: He'll just *become*.

RITA: Like for the first time.

SAL: It's the best we can do.

(RITA *and* SAL *sit for a moment.* VAL *continues to nurse.*)

RITA: Shall we begin?

SAL: Yes.

(RITA *leans down and whispers gently to the baby as he continues to suckle.*)

RITA: Photosynthesis, Val. The conversion of water, energy and carbon dioxide into oxygen.

(RITA *looks to* SAL.)

SAL: Tell him what you know, Rita.

RITA: Abraham was the father of the Jews. Through the faith he showed in his willingness to slay his son on the peak of Mount Moriah, a covenant of plenty and fecundity was established between God and the Israelites. (*Beat*) Christ was a very good man. He was possibly the son of God and died for our sins. But of He, you shall learn plenty later on.

(SAL—*still staring out*)

SAL: Muslims.

RITA: Mohammed was born in Mecca in 570 A D. He later went to Yathrib and renamed it Medina. He preached the five basic principles, as revealed to him by Gabriel, and from the peak of Mount Moriah, he ascended to heaven on a winged horse.

SAL: He just needs an overview, Rita.

RITA: The Mormons were founded by Joseph Smith, they enjoy blood atonement and most people consider them a bit nutty but there are a lot of them out there and we should respect all people.

SAL: The Witnesses.

RITA: Jehovah's Witnesses are *legitimately* nutty but that's not really our business. In the beginning, there was light, which ties in with the photosynthesis.

SAL: *(To* VAL*)* E = Mc-squared.

RITA: Your father's very scientific.

SAL: Cogito Ergo Sum. The truth shall set you free, Right over might, nothing to fear but fear itself; vive la resistance, everything in moderation, the buck stops here; love thy neighbor, pie is twenty-two sevenths, Anne Frank, Ben Franklin, Barney Frank, Frankenstein. Life is strife, Pinocchio lies, and no matter what— always be an individual, responsible for your own actions.

RITA: To look good is to feel good.

SAL: *(Objecting)* Rita—

RITA: He needs to know it all. *(Back to* VAL*)* Also, we live in an geodesic, indeterminate universe where space is curvilinear and all potential substance and meaning is ultimately indefinable, a jumble of quarks, a gaggle of neutrinos.

SAL: There were many good Native Americans who got a bad deal, including Squanto and Geronimo. And of course the Blacks were treated terribly in this country, which is why we honor Nat Turner, Paul Robeson, Martin Luther King.... *(He can think of no more)*

RITA: C'mon, Sal—

SAL: Jackie Robinson.

RITA: Keep going—

SAL: —*Calvin Coolidge.*

RITA: No, dear.

SAL: He just *sounds* so Black.

RITA: *(Standing)* That's it for today.

(RITA *puts down the baby, and from now on speaks to* VAL, *who joins his parents as he quickly gets dressed.* VAL *is a young man whose demeanor should remain essentially the same for the rest of the play, i.e. he should not "play" his age—which is continuously in motion—any more than with subtle mannerisms and the occasional costume piece.)*

SAL: Okay, son, it's your first day of school and I want you to knock 'em dead. And remember, don't take long walks on short piers, this too shall pass, and all men are created equal. Basically. Got it?

VAL: Yes, sir.

SAL: Good. Off you go. Take the Ho Chi Minh to the Trail of Tears, left on the information highway, right on Jack Lalane, left on Easy Street, back on My Way, you take the high road, straight on through to the other side. You really can't miss it.

RITA: Impress your teacher with the Monroe Doctrine, Wilson's 14 points, the democratically-assured freedom of assemblage and John Brown at Harper's Ferry. Off you go.

SAL: *(Taking him by the shoulders, speaking directly)* And don't forget: *Fight for what you believe.*

(VAL *nods, turns to go)*

SAL: *(Calling after him)* Unless you move to Switzerland, which is a valiant nation that believes in peace at all costs!—*as well as* anonymous banking!

(VAL *walks over to school, where his teacher*, MR RHEUM, *awaits him. Also in school are three mates*, NEW, PRO *and* RUDI. RHEUM *performs the following ditty accompanied by a tight drum beat*)

RHEUM:
Hi there, Val, welcome to your school
I'm here to teach you logic and a slice of golden rule
Certain things your parents said are quite completely
    wrong
I'll now correct just some of them, with my little song
As to all this nonsense apropos "thou shalt not kill"
Survival of the fittest seems to put that all to nil
We kill each other daily, it's a form of re-baptism
But all of it is legal because it's called cap-i-ta-lism
And as for that big lie that in the beginning there was
    light
I'd like to set the record straight by stating it was night
Nothingness was ruler and around it darkness hung
The concept of humanity had yet to have begun
Our humble little universe was just an ole black hole
Until the Big Bang came along to set us on a roll

(*Drums end with a tiny flourish*)

RHEUM: Any questions?

NEW: (*Raising his hand*) Yes. What else?

RHEUM: Well of course there's peace on earth, good will towards man, man bites dog, the dog ate my homework, eight minutes for light to get to earth, light is energy, energy makes us sexually active, it's good to be sexually active so long as your mother's not making your bed. One has to cut the cord. On that note, don't fantasize about sleeping with your mothers—unless you're in a jam and it's really necessary. On the Oedipal note, our society is based on the irresistible impetus of profit motive which is really just a polite way of saying, "Love me, Mother, love me", but profit

is legal and mother-boinking's not so we have to
watch our step. In addition, we hold these truths to be
self-evident: "just do it", "go for it", "get it while you
can", "good will towards Mom" —Hey but seriously!
—As for fathers—certain of you will feel guilty-as
you grow—for the things they did and the evil they
bequeathed; you'll read history, be spat at, see the light
and recover memories. All of that's to be expected—for
fathers are the essential source of all bigotry and greed
in this world. I'm just here to reinforce that. By the
way, America doesn't play favorites when it comes to
religion, meaning the municipal crèche must cost the
same as the municipal Menorah. As for the Muslims—
nice folks but too much Jihad, not enough Ramadan;
Jehovah's Witnesses—absolute nutjobs but give `em
credit for not saluting the flag— *(Muttering)* —fucking
commies. Okay! —Have a nice night and don't believe
everything your parents tell you, especially that one
about Abraham and Isaac, because the fact is, the Abe-
man was ready to annihilate that old biblical favorite
"thou shalt not kill". Talk about a mixed message from
Dad. Can't have your cake and kill your son. Just goes
to show you, who woulda thunk! Okay—off you go!

(School breaks up and VAL *is approached by a young girl,*
RUDI; *a young boy,* NEW; *and a young girl,* PRO*)*

NEW: What's up?

VAL: What's up.

NEW: Did you know the Gestapo was evil?

VAL: No.

NEW: They are.

VAL: Oh.

PRO: *(To* NEW*)* He probably doesn't even know about
the Good War.

NEW: *(To* VAL*)* Did you know there was a Good War?

VAL: *(Faking)* I've heard about it.

NEW: Who was in it?

VAL: Us and them.

NEW: Who was them?

VAL: *(Guessing)* The Gestapo.

PRO: Lucky guess.

RUDI: Lay off him. He's cool.

NEW: He's a nerd

RUDI: What's your name?

VAL: Val.

RUDI: What kind of name is that?

VAL: It comes from the hardware store.

PRO: Which one?

VAL: True Value.

RUDI: I like that. It's cool.

VAL: Thanks.

RUDI: So Val, do you know about photosynthesis?

VAL: Sure, it's CO_2 plus light plus water equals oxygen.

RUDI: *(To others)* I told you he was legit. You wanna hang with us?

VAL: I was taught to be an individual.

RUDI: Don't worry about it, our group's *into* individuality.

VAL: Cool.

RUDI: My name's Rudi and this is New and Pro.

VAL: *(Shaking hands)* Hey.

PRO &NEW: Hey.

NEW: You oughta tell him, Rudi.

RUDI: Oh yeah, we don't believe in God.

(VAL *looks down and shuffles his feet.*)

RUDI: Is that a problem?

VAL: I was told not to question God's existence until college.

PRO: *(To others)* Yo, he's way out of it.

RUDI: It's not like that anymore, Val. We waited 'til second grade to question Him and even *then* we were considered nerds.

VAL: But I'm still in second.

NEW: Then don't hang with us.

VAL: No, I'll hang with you. I was gonna question Him this summer anyway. Plus, my parents aren't really sure about Him. They think He's flawed.

RUDI: Yeah, well we think He's a complete and utter non-entity, but either way, cool—you're in.

VAL: Thanks.

RUDI: See you tomorrow, Val.

VAL: See you.

(The others exit, VAL *turns back into his bedroom. He sees* RITA *making his bed)*

VAL: Mom, stop!

RITA: What for, honey?

VAL: You shouldn't do that. I can make my own bed.

RITA: I really don't mind.

VAL: But I have to cut the cord!

(SAL *comes home from work.*)

SAL: Hi, honey, I'm home! Hi there, Val, how was school?

VAL: Our society is based on the irresistible impetus for profit motive.

SAL: You bet your bottom dollar it is, but that doesn't mean we can't give generously to the ill-nourished, ill-clad and ill-housed, as well as have deep sympathy for all those left behind.

VAL: Did you make money today, Dad?

SAL: I sure as hell did, son. Fair day's wages for a fair day's work. And by the way: All the news that's fit to print and oh yes, God have mercy on the poor and wretched souls of the earth.

VAL: I was thinking that maybe God doesn't exist, Dad.

SAL: Now don't say that, Val, of course God exists, it's just that He's sublimely wedged within the splendid minutiae of our everyday lives. He's in the details.

VAL: He is?

SAL: Sure, wedged right in the minutiae. He's in that perfectly constructed bird's nest on the branch of the great oak out back, He's in the way someone's voice falters slightly when they're telling their life story. Yes siree, God's in the details much more than He's in heaven. *That's* what you need to remember.

VAL: Dad, tell me about the Good War.

SAL: *(Sudden and decisive)* I don't want to talk about it.

VAL: But you fought in it, didn't you?

SAL: *(Loud)* I don't want to talk about it!

RITA: *(Entering)* He's just being modest, Val.

SAL: Fight for what you believe in, son.

RITA: Your father was a hero but heroes don't like to brag.

SAL: *(Reprimandingly)* Rita—

VAL: Why was he a hero, Mom. Did he kill the Gestapo?

RITA: He sure did. He killed two hundred Gestapo, fifty-six kamikazes, twenty-seven Italians and two handicapped Persians who he mistook for Bavarian.

VAL: Wow, Dad—

SAL: Son, if you'd like to hear about how the wild wild west was won only to end up as Sacramento, that I can do, but otherwise, I don't wanna talk about it.

VAL: That's okay—

SAL: Or if you'd like to hear about the self-correcting character of American democracy—

VAL: No thank you—

RITA: What are you doing, Val?

(VAL *has found a book of matches and is lighting them.*)

VAL: Nothing.

RITA: Don't play with matches.

VAL: Why not?

RITA: Because if kids play with matches then they'll dream of fire and soon they'll be wetting their bed in a subconscious effort to put the fire out.

(*Off* SAL'*s inquisitive look:*)

RITA: Freud.

SAL: (*To* VAL) Okay—back to school for you, kiddo!

(VAL *returns to school, joined by his friends,* NEW, PRO *and* RUDI.)

NEW: What's up, True Value?

VAL: Not much. How're you guys?

RUDI: We're good, both as individuals and as a group.

VAL: Good.

RUDI: Did you learn anything since we last hung out?

VAL: Yes. I learned that God is wedged in the splendid minutiae.

PRO: Who taught you *that* shit?

VAL: My father.

RUDI: No offense, Val, but is this the same father who told you to love thy neighbor?

VAL: Yes.

NEW: What if your neighbor was a Gestapo?

VAL: I'm not sure.

PRO: Okay then.

RUDI: No one said it would be easy, Val.

VAL: I guess not. Hey, by the way, I've been meaning to ask you guys what your names are short for.

NEW: We didn't choose them. They were forced upon us.

VAL: I know, I'm just curious.

NEW: *(Pause)* New is short for New Deal. And Pro...tell him, Pro.

PRO: Progressive Era.

RUDI: Are you gonna pay attention in class today, Val?

VAL: Should I?

RUDI: It's your call; but just so you know—*we're* not.

(The four friends are now in class with RHEUM, *their backs turned to him)*

RHEUM: *(Handing out baseball helmets and bats)* Okay, kids, baseball! Originally a fertility ritual for thirteen-year old Mesopotamian girls, now a billion dollar business full of men who like to *date* thirteen year-

old girls. Val, you're up. Rudi, you can be my special
assistant.

(VAL *puts a helmet on his head and steps up to the plate.*
NEW *assumes catcher's position and* RHEUM *pitches, with*
RUDI *at his side.* RHEUM *tosses* VAL *a ball,* VAL *hits it out
of the theater. As he drops the bat,* RUDI, *having watched in
awe, steps up to him.*)

RUDI: I think I'm falling for you, Val.

VAL: Why?

RUDI: I don't know. Baseball's an unimaginably boring
game......and yet there's something about it that
makes you beautiful.

RHEUM: I think Walt Whitman put it best when he
said, "It's America's game. It has the snap, go and
fling of the American atmosphere; it belongs to our
institutions, fits into them like our constitution's laws."
(Flirtatious) Huh, Rudi?

RUDI: *(Entranced by* VAL*)* I don't think that's it, Mr.
Rheum.

VAL: *(To* RUDI*)* You're nice.

RUDI: So are you.

VAL: So are you.

RUDI: Will you go with me, Val?

VAL: Where?

RUDI: Just......go.

VAL: Yes.

(VAL *and* RUDI *kiss shyly on the cheek as others watch.
Suddenly,* RITA *and* SAL *are there.*)

RITA: Val!

VAL: Mom?!

RITA: Get in the car.

VAL: What car?

SAL: We have a brand new car now, son. Big tail fins.

VAL: *(To* RUDI*)* I'll talk to you later.

(Others disappear.)

RITA: *(Urgent)* We don't do premarital sex in this family, Val.

VAL: But I wasn't!

RITA: Talk to your father.

VAL: Dad?

SAL: Get it while you can, son.

RITA: Sal!

SAL: I mean—how old are you, son?

VAL: Almost thirteen.

SAL: And you like this girl?

VAL: I love her.

SAL: Son, nobody knows what love is. It's an ultimately elusive concept.

RITA: Sal!

SAL: What I'm trying to say is that sex is bad. Unless you've had some sort of…Bedouin ceremony.

VAL: I wasn't having sex.

SAL: You weren't?

VAL: No!

SAL: Why not?

VAL: Because we just fell in love *today*!

SAL: Continue—

VAL: And we have to give the relationship time to mature.

SAL: Ah huh—

VAL: What is it you want to tell me, Dad?

SAL: Rita?

RITA: The act of intercourse is a sacred event. It should take place in a secure and loving environment at a time when the participants are sure they want to spend the rest of their lives together.

VAL: Is that how you and Dad were?

RITA: To an extent.

VAL: Well I *do* want to spend the rest of my life with Rudi and I would never force her to do anything she's not ready for and I agree that we should wait until we're married; or engaged; or thinking about it.

SAL: Okay let's go for that drive!

(RITA *and* SAL *exit,* VAL *starts to follow them when he is called with a loud whisper by* RUDI.)

RUDI: Val!

VAL: *(Turning back)* Yes?

RUDI: What was that about?

VAL: They want us to refrain from premarital sex.

RUDI: Why?

VAL: They say it's a sacred act.

RUDI: Do you agree?

VAL: …I don't know.

RUDI: Me neither. *(Pause)* What if I told you I love you?

VAL: I would say I love you, too.

RUDI: Then I think we should try.

VAL: But my parents disapprove.

RUDI: We wouldn't have to go all the way. It's like baseball: We could hit triples and still be happy. *(Honest)* Besides, we're in love.

(RUDI *takes* VAL's *hand…from offstage*)

SAL: Let's go, Val! The Chevy's waiting!

VAL: I have to go.

RUDI: Think about it.

VAL: I will. (*He turns, then back*) A lot.

(VAL *exits, leaving* RUDI *alone on stage. A moment later, she is joined by* PRO. *They look after* VAL *in the distance.*)

PRO: All men are created equal.

RUDI: Not that one.

PRO: He *is* cute.

RUDI: Hey—

PRO: By the people, of the people, for the people.

RUDI: Don't triangulate me, Pro.

PRO: All I'm saying is, I think he's cute.

RUDI: Thou shalt not covet thy neighbor's wife.

PRO: I'm not your neighbor and he's not your wife.

(PRO *exits as the scene shifts to* VAL's *house, where* RITA, SAL *and* VAL *eat dinner.*)

SAL: Val, did your mother and I ever tell you that life isn't always fair?

VAL: Yes, Dad.

SAL: Did we ever advise you that you should ask not what your country can do for you, but—

VAL: —What you can do for your country. Yes.

SAL: Good. (*Beat*) And the birds and the bees?

VAL: No, Dad.

SAL: (*To self*) Fuck.

RITA: Do we have to have this conversation while I'm eating pork chops?

SAL: I think it's best, Rita. Val's reached an age where we can no longer afford to keep him in the dark. Would you like to start?

RITA: No.

SAL: Fine. Val, the penis goes into the vagina, try not to leave it in there for too long or you might get stuck. Other than that, a good, steady rhythm is your best bet. If she instructs you to do anything more specific, it's usually in your best interest to immediately comply. Anything you'd like to add, Rita?

RITA: No, dear.

SAL: Okay then. Apple sauce, Val?

(As VAL *turns to go,* RITA *calls softly.*)

RITA: Val.

VAL: Yes, Mom?

RITA: *(Pause)* Love.

VAL: …What do you mean?

RITA: *(Her hand on her heart) Love.*

(VAL *is now mowing the lawn with a hand mower. It is very hot out and his shirt is off. He pauses and writes a letter in his head which we hear as a voice over.*)

VAL: *(V O)* "Dear Rudi, you are all that I have ever thought about for three weeks now. Your hair curls around the corners of my mind, a stray strand falling onto my cortex, insinuating its way into my perception of the world, making me happier than I ever imagined I could be. I want to be with you, Rudi, just that, collecting your hair until I have a wig that I can wear inside my scalp. Sincerely, and with love pouring through my sweat pores—Val."

(*By the end of the letter,* RUDI *has entered the yard*)

RUDI: I loved your poem.

VAL: It was a letter.

RUDI: It was a poem.

VAL: You're nice.

RUDI: So are you. *(Quiet)* You're special. I mean, everyone's special, but……you're *you*. Like no one else. *(Comes closer)* Can anybody see us back here?

VAL: I'm not sure.

RUDI: Then we should work quickly.

VAL: What're we going to do?

RUDI: *(Approaching him slowly)* Vectorial and topological geometry. Synergetic energy…

VAL: …in a curvilinear universe?

RUDI: …Love…

(As music plays, they embrace gently and deeply……as Lights shift)

(VAL and NEW in their baseball uniforms, both swinging bats)

NEW: Word has it you hit a homer the other day.

VAL: You shouldn't talk like that, New.

NEW: It's nothing to be ashamed of. I'm envious.

VAL: I love her.

NEW: You gonna marry her?

VAL: Yeah.

NEW: You sure?

VAL: I think.

NEW: Good.

(VAL and NEW are suddenly distracted by something in the distance)

NEW: There goes that new girl.

VAL: Who?

NEW: Boom-Boom. She's a *fine* glass of *wine*.

VAL: Boom-Boom?

NEW: You know— Booming Economy.

VAL: Oh.

NEW: *(Beat; they swing bats.)* So, does Rudi have a nice grassy knoll?

VAL: What does that mean?

NEW: You know, *grassy knoll.*

VAL: No I don't.

NEW: The second shooter...the unaccounted for trajectory...

(VAL doesn't get it.)

NEW: You know— *Grassy knoll,* man!

VAL: Oh.

NEW: Does she?

VAL: *(Pause shy)* I'd say it's more...*turfy?*

(NEW slaps him on the back and exits. VAL stands alone. PRO enters.)

PRO: Hey, Val.

VAL: Oh, hey Pro.

PRO: Hey.

VAL: What's going on?

PRO: I heard you're in love with Rudi.

VAL: Yeah.

PRO: Why?

VAL: Why what?

PRO: Why are you in love with *her?*

VAL: I guess I just am.

PRO: Was it because she was the first one there?

VAL: I don't know.

PRO: Because guess what.

VAL: What?

PRO: *(Honest, simple)* I love you too.

VAL: Really?

PRO: Really. And it's not that I'm trying to be competitive, either. Because I've always loved you. Even *before* you played baseball. But I didn't know what love was. I thought it was......something else. But it was love.

VAL: For me?

PRO: Yes.

VAL: I had no idea.

PRO: That's usually how it is. *(Approaching him)* Rudi's my best friend, but I don't think she loves you like I do.

VAL: Maybe you both love me the same.

PRO: Maybe. *(Closing in on him)* But there's something I learned that maybe she doesn't know.

VAL: What is it?

PRO: You have to promise not to tell the others.

VAL: I promise.

PRO: *(Simple)* "If I am not for myself, then who is for me? If I am for myself alone, then what am I? If not now, when?"

VAL: *(Touched)* What does it mean?

PRO: It means believe in yourself but don't be selfish. And it means you should always act on your beliefs. *(Very close)* Do you think you could love me back?

VAL: But I love Rudi.

PRO: That's not what I asked. *(Closer)* Do you think you could love me?

VAL: *(Honest)* Yes.

PRO: Good

(VAL *and* PRO *kiss, it lasts and is quite beautiful and simple. No music, just silence......until* RUDI *walks in)*

RUDI: Val?

(The kiss ends.)

RUDI: Pro?

VAL: Rudi—

RUDI: How could you?

VAL: She loves me.

RUDI: Do you love her?

VAL: Yes.

RUDI: Do you love me?

VAL: Yes.

RUDI: You can't love us both, Val!

VAL: Why not?

RUDI: Because it's not cool!

VAL: But it's true.

PRO: Deal with it, Rudi.

RUDI: It's not cool and you guys know it.

PRO: So what're you gonna do?

RUDI: I'll leave.

VAL: Don't, Rudi—

RUDI: We made love, Val. Don't you understand what that means?

VAL: It means I love you.

RUDI: Yes—

VAL: So what's wrong?

(RUDI *cannot answer, for she is crying. Her tears are not loud, but rather soft and profound, reflecting both this moment and something beyond......as the scene shifts and others enter.*)

RHEUM: It is my honor to now introduce this year's salutatorian, the one and only Val Jones!

(PRO, NEW, SAL *and* RITA *applaud as* RHEUM *stands behind* RUDI, *giving her a massage.* VAL *stands at a podium and addresses the crowd hesitantly, but by the end is focused only on* RUDI.)

VAL: Parents. teachers, fellow classmates, we have learned many things over our years together. We have learned to love. Perhaps too much. (*Beat*) But can there really be such a thing as too much love? It sounds strange. (*Pause*) I'm sorry if I've hurt people in my life. If I could trade my salutatorian-ship for having not done this, I would, because people shouldn't hurt people, even if it means they're not able to love as much. Or maybe people should learn to love in a more economical way. I suppose that's what I've learned here at General Schwartzkopf High School. To love—wisely. (*Pause*) I guess what I'm trying to say is that, yes, love is the *answer*, but sometimes the *question* is quite complex. (*Pause*) Thank you, everybody, for helping to teach me that. (*He starts to leave, then stops. Very simple:*) Oh yeah— Go Beavers.

(*The ceremony breaks up, people hug each other.* VAL *finds* RUDI *alone in the corner, as others gradually exit.*)

VAL: Hey, Rudi.

RUDI: Hey. (*Beat*) Nice speech.

VAL: Really?

RUDI: *(Feigning ambivalence)* Yeah.

VAL: Do you think we'll still see each other after today?

RUDI: I don't know. Aren't you going to college?

VAL: Yeah, aren't you?

RUDI: Nope.

VAL: Oh.

(VAL and RUDI shuffle their feet a moment.)

VAL: I still love you.

RUDI: Yeah. Me and Pro.

VAL: I don't think I really love Pro. I mean, I did for a minute or two. I really did. But then it stopped. But it never stopped with you.

RUDI: Why?

VAL: Because you always know what you want. And who you are.

RUDI: *(Pause)* Well, we'll see what happens. I'm not really into love right now anyway.

VAL: Okay.

(RUDI exits. VAL stands alone. RICH, an American wearing a Nazi uniform—played by actor #3—enters. We should not recognize him as any other character.)

RICH: Hey.

VAL: Hey.

RICH: Nice speech.

VAL: Really?

RICH: Yeah. Uplifting.

VAL: *(Beat)* Are you a Nazi?

RICH: Yeah.

VAL: Gestapo?

RICH: No, no, no— No Gestapo here.

(Awkward silence. VAL is confused.)

VAL: So you were just here for the—

RICH: The graduation—yeah. I always try and make 'em.

VAL: Do I know you?

RICH: Oh, I'm sorry— *(Hand held out)* I'm Rich; Rich *Wiednerheindler*! Nice to meet you.

VAL: *(Shaking)* You too.

RICH: Hey, you know what? —You should never shake hands with a Nazi. People see you doing that, they'll give you major flak.

VAL: You're probably right.

RICH: Ya. *(Beat)* Hey, one land, one people.

(VAL is unsure how to react.)

RICH: All right. I'll be seeing you.

VAL: Bye.

(RICH exits.)

Scene 2

(VAL goes to college. A sudden and abrupt scene change— accompanied by drums and a slight, perhaps misguided, light show)

(PROFESSOR SEBUM—actor #3—a middle-aged, bohemian man with an in-your-face conviction as to the validity of his words, sings to VAL and others—actors #5 and #6)

SEBUM:
It's bullshit, it's bullshit,
Everything you've learned, up to now

It's horseshit, it's donkey-ass-shit
If you thought it was a lion, it's really just a cow
Hey you sittin' there with that hope upon your face
If you think that life is simple you must be from outer
    space
Now that you're in college, there are things you must
    explore
Roosevelt had a mistress, and Kennedy was a whore
But that's really just the surface of the knowledge
    you'll receive
For the point of higher learning is to doubt what you
    perceive
Here's one more example that you really ought to
    know
Lincoln freed the slaves as a political side-show
And on the topic of revision, let us look a bit more near
For if God is so damn gentle, why are humans full of
    fear?

SEBUM: *(Continuing)* Which brings us to Kierkegaard's
Fear and Trembling, which, as you know, deals with the
story of Abraham and Isaac. A man *commanded* by God
to sacrifice his son so as to demonstrate his faith. Now
sure, there are those who say that by pulling a double-
edged saber on his own flesh and blood, Abraham
screwed his son up for life. "Hey, Dad, I'm your son,
not the family goat." But what *I'm* saying is—the
man *acted* on his beliefs. He may have been a chump,
he may have screwed up his son, he may even have
believed in a God that doesn't exist, but the fact is, he
acted on his convictions. And I dig that. I really do,

(Snaps all around)

SEBUM: I dig the *hellity-hell* out of it. Okay. Billy, let's
hear your report.

(BILLY—*actor #5*—*reads from his report as the song,
accompanied on his boom box by the song,* I Believe I Can
Fly.)

BILLY: "Here's what *I* think is right." By Billy. "We
the people hold these truths to be self-evident: That
the hopes and dreams of this nation were stowaway
passengers on the spaceship Challenger, and thus
that nice little teacher from New Hampshire was not
the only thing to Live Free and Die. Along with her
were Chris Columbus, organized religion, manifest
destiny, white man's burden, the train tracks leading
to Auschwitz, Hiroshima as a 'military base,' 'Houston
we have a problem," the constitution—which is a
covenant with death and an agreement with hell—and
the 'Declaration of Whatever The Fuck He Was Talking
About!'"

(The song blows up and ends.)

BILLY: Why, might you ask, have I reached these
shattering conclusions? Because the old truth no longer
lives, it will *not* set you free because the *new* truth is
that righteousness leads to dogma! And that's what
happened here: A country by *some* of the people, of
some of the people, for *some* of the people! Thus spoke
Zarathustra!

SEBUM: Good job, son.

BILLY: I ain't your son.

SEBUM: Good job, Billy.

(BILLY *sits.*)

SEBUM: Anyone want to add anything?

VAL: *(Hesitant)* It sounds a little harsh.

BILLY: *Fuck you, homeboy!*

SEBUM: I think what Billy's trying to say is that he feels
he has a right to express his opinion that America

hasn't lived up to all its ideals, and that if you disagree you can formulate your own thesis.

VAL: It's not that I disagree, I just think we have to remember to love one another.

SEBUM: You can't love if you don't know what hate is.

VAL: Really?

SEBUM: Absolutely. What do *you* hate, Val?

VAL: I'm not sure.

SEBUM: Think about it, do you hate your Mom?

VAL: No.

SEBUM: You sure?

VAL: Yes.

SEBUM: Give it some more thought.

(SEBUM, *handing* VAL *a computer:*)

SEBUM: Here, use this, it'll give you time to think about the big questions, because you see, God doesn't exist, meaning even if you *build it*, the motherfucker won't come. And if he did, he's *certainly* not gonna "sublimely wedge himself in the splendid minutiae." Leave the minutiae to the computer, use your time to ponder the *big* questions. *Be your OWN God.* Okay Willa, let's hear it.

(WILLA, *played by actor #6, stands and delivers her report.*)

WILLA: Now that we have shrugged off the slavish morality of Judeo-Christian imprisonment and are able to openly acknowledge that Thornton Wilder was a homo, I think we need to reinterpret the body of his work. *Our Town* should be a gay fantasia SPECTACLE with K D Lang as stage manager, Ling Ling as George, and Tom Cruise as Emily!

SEBUM: Is that it?

WILLA: No. *(Fist raised)* FREE PUERTO RICO!!

SEBUM: Good job, Willa.

WILLA: *Suck my ass, fucker!*

SEBUM: Great! In closing, I'd just like to say that during the next few weeks, you will be asked to join frats and sororities, at which you might find yourself calling out for advice: "Why, if George Washington was a Freemason, can't *I* be in a frat?" But only *you* can answer. Only *you* can shrug off conformity; only *you* can act with conviction. *(He looks at his watch)* Have a good afternoon, and remember, don't believe everything you learned in high school, for this too shall pass.

(Class breaks up, all leave but for VAL, *who stays seated, confused, and* WILLA, *who watches him for a moment before speaking.)*

Will: Hey.

VAL: Hey.

WILLA: Do you wanna have sex?

VAL: Why?

WILLA: Cause.

VAL: Okay.

*(*WILLA *goes to* VAL, *sits on him.)*

WILLA: It's good?

VAL: Yes.

WILLA: Why?

VAL: I don't know.

WILLA: Because you're not in high school anymore. Didn't you hear what the Professor said? It's time to have some fun.

VAL: But what about love?

WILLA: That's what we're doing.

VAL: *(Trance-like)* Make love, not war.

(With this, VAL tentatively places his hand on WILLA's breast)

WILLA: Unconditional surrender…

(VAL and WILLA kiss; he gains confidence.)

VAL: …I think there's a silent majority between my legs.

WILLA: …I've got a U N mandate to goose your fuckin' moose.

(Gaining momentum)

VAL: Battle of the Bulge.

WILLA: Battle for Midway.

(VAL and WILLA are now kissing, their bodies writhing)

VAL: *…Habeus corpus ex post facto.…*

WILLA: *…Don't need a weatherman to know which way the wind blows.…*

VAL: *…First thought, best thought.…*

Will: *…Last train to Clarksville!*

VAL: *…Sum es est, sumus estes sunt!!*

WILLA: *…Magna cum laude!!!*

VAL: *IF YOU BUILD IT HE WON'T CUM!!!*

WILLA: *CUM BAY YAA!!*

VAL: *COITUS INTERRUPTUS!!!.……*

(VAL and WILLA stop)

VAL: Shit.

WILLA: You didn't.

(VAL nods dejectedly.)

WILLA: You're supposed to wait for me.

VAL: I tried.

WILLA: Don't sweat it.

(WILLA *continues to grind her thighs on* VAL'*s legs until—thoroughly satisfied—she climbs off.*)

WILLA: *(Exiting)* E R A, douchebag.

(VAL *is left alone on stage. A moment later, a big, blond, flirtatious Dolly Parton-look-alike wearing a Nazi uniform—actor #4—strolls by.*)

DOLLY: Hey.

VAL: Hey.

DOLLY: Nine to five.

VAL: What a way to make a living?

DOLLY: Barely getting by.

VAL: All taking and no giving?

DOLLY: *(Exiting)* You betcha.

(VAL *regards* DOLLY *curiously. She is gone. He speaks to his parents on the phone. They stand opposite.*)

VAL: Mom?

RITA: Hi, darling, how are you?!

VAL: I'm a little homesick.

RITA: But are you having a good time?

VAL: I think so.

RITA: Then you're not homesick.

VAL: I think I'm both.

RITA: That's impossible, honey. Now listen, you're there to learn. Everything else is irrelevant. Tell me what you've learned.

VAL: I learned that the Good War wasn't so good.

SAL: Of course it was good, don't believe those bohemian freaks who spend their time smoking pot and wishing they had a farm. You know the saying, "If you can't do it, teach it", and that's all they are. You just make sure you get a degree, I'm paying through my ass for that college.

RITA: Now don't pay attention to your grumpy old father, his pendulum is swinging and he's not wearing briefs. Okay then? Hugs and kisses and remember, always, *love*.

(*A demented* BARTENDER, *played by Actor #3, enters with a six pack of Budweiser, placing it down in front of* VAL)

BART: What'll it be?

(VAL *regards the six pack*)

VAL: Bud.

BART: Coming right up.

(BART *peels a Bud off the six pack and hands it to* VAL.)

BART: Fifteen bucks.

(VAL *pays* BART, *drinks as much of it as he can.*)

BART: You college kids think you got it rough.

VAL: Yeah.

BART: Well lemme just tell you something, you don't know rough. Try seeing the world for what it is.

VAL: What is it?

BART: It's rough. Try workin' for a living, you little shit.

VAL: But I'm in college.

BART: Exactly—try *not* going to college, try spending your youth cutting galvanized steel with acetylene torches in the Brooklyn shipyard, breathing in zinc shards, coming down with cancer when you're forty-six years old. *That's* rough, you little turd—zinc shards in your lungs. College is a bowl of fucking cherries!

VAL: Why are you mad at me?

BART: Because I'm sick and tired of being sick and tired of people like you. Now drink your beer and go jump off a building.

(BART *leaves and* VAL *picks up the other beers and slowly walks back to his dorm room. On the way, he passes a bench where a young couple is heavily entwined. He watches for a moment before recognizing one)*

VAL: Willa?

(WILLA *turns around;* VAL *recognizes the second person.)*

VAL: Billy?

BILLY: What's up, Val-U-mart?

VAL: *(To* WILLA*)* I thought we were a thing?

WILLA: We are. I have a *lot* of things.

BILLY: You can come back for leftovers, Valley, if there *are* any.

(BILLY *and* WILLA *resume their entwinement.)*

VAL: *(Quietly)* But I thought we would be in love.

(No answer. Beats. VAL *continues watching them, sadness overtaking him.......as* BILLY *and* WILLA *fade away.* VAL *now stands alone, still holding his beers. He opens another and drinks it all.* SEBUM *enters)*

SEBUM: Hi there, Val.

VAL: Hello, Professor Sebum.

SEBUM: May I have some of that beer?

VAL: Sure.

(VAL *hands a beer to* SEBUM.)*

SEBUM: How's college treating you?

VAL: Okay.

SEBUM: If you're not a Marxist by twenty, you have no heart, if you're not a capitalist by thirty, you have no brain.

VAL: I'm not sure what I am.

SEBUM: That's okay, just don't join a frat.

(VAL *watches* SEBUM *chug his beer.*)

VAL: Professor Sebum?

SEBUM: *(With a burp)* Yeah?

VAL: *(Child-like in his naiveté)* Do you think I'm a conformist?

SEBUM: Of course you are, son; nothing to worry about.

VAL: But you told us today to question what we've been taught and shrug off conformity.

SEBUM: Yes, Val, that was *rhetoric*.

VAL: But didn't you mean it?

SEBUM: Only in so much as I said it.

VAL: I don't understand.

SEBUM: It's the nature of the beast. Once you get here, we teach you how to think radically, but all in the same way. We make you read important books, each one penned by us; we teach you words of revolution to blaze you up the corporate ladder; we homogenize your argumentative skills so that you'll hate each other smoothly; teach you to run so that you may eventually stand still; pour the beer freely so as to extinguish moral fear; and promise you lots of income so that you'll repay your loans with interest.

VAL: So then why are you here?

SEBUM: Good dental. *(Opens another beer)* But if I were you, before you go any further in debt, before you find a little wifey and kids, before you learn the revolution by rote—if I were you, I'd take a sac full of books and be gone, be gone with thee, before the establishment gets inside your bones.

(VAL *watches as* SEBUM *finishes his second beer.*)

SEBUM: Thanks for the beer.

(SEBUM *exits.* VAL *exits in the other direction.*)

Scene 3

(RITA *and* SAL *sit in the living room of the house where* VAL *grew up.* RITA *is noticeably younger than she was,* SAL *noticeably older.*)

SAL: My God, woman, you grow more beautiful by the year.

RITA: It's just vitamins, Sal. If you took yours like I tell you, you'd have the same youthful glow.

SAL: What's the point, my youth was a failure.

RITA: It wasn't your fault, Sal—

SAL: I don't want to talk about it.

RITA: You're a good man.

SAL: *(Hard of hearing)* What?

RITA: I said, "You're a good man"!

SAL: It's worse than it's ever been.

RITA: What is?

SAL: The ears. Worse everyday

(VAL *enters carrying a large sac of books and his remaining two beers.*)

VAL: Hello Mom, hello Dad.

SAL: Why are you here, son?

VAL: I've dropped out of college.

SAL: The hell you have!

RITA: What happened, Val?

VAL: I just...it wasn't working for me.

SAL: What the hell does that mean?

VAL: I can study on my own. Look— *(Opening his bag)* I have all the books.

SAL: Excuse me, but I didn't eat butter sandwiches for twenty years for *this!*

(RITA and VAL look at SAL in confusion)

SAL: I didn't fight in the Good War in order to get the G I Bill in order to get an education in order to get a job in order to save money in order to send you to college in order to have you walk back in here a year later with a sac full of books and a pithy explanation!

RITA: Sal, don't exaggerate—

SAL: I've got this under control, Rita.

VAL: I'm an adult, Dad, I can think for myself.

SAL: Oh really? What is it that you think?

VAL: I think for myself.

SAL: Yes, but what *exactly* is it that you are now so profoundly thinking??

VAL: I don't want the establishment to get inside my bones.

SAL: Ohhhh.

VAL: I'm trying to act on my conviction my convictions.

SAL: Which are what?

VAL: Which are that maybe God doesn't exist at all.

(RITA gasps.)

SAL: *(To* RITA*)* That's all right, honey, he's been in college.

VAL: And that maybe love *isn't* the answer.

RITA: *(Standing)* Oh dear God.

SAL: I see. And how did you come to that brilliant conclusion?

VAL: Experience.

SAL: Ohhhh—

VAL: Yes. And now it's time for me to experience the *real* world, where life isn't a bowl of cherries and there are zinc shards in my lungs.

SAL: Good. But don't plan on doing any of that around here, because we're fresh out of zinc shards and we *don't* take college drop-outs!

VAL: You're not going to let me stay here?

(No answer)

VAL: Mom?

RITA: Your father has a point, Val. If you want to experience life without the cherries, you should find your own bowl.

*(*VAL *picks up his bag and beer, starts to leave.)*

RITA: Val?

*(*VAL *stops,* RITA *goes to him and hugs him. Reluctantly,* SAL *stands.)*

SAL: This hurts me more than it hurts you. *(He hugs* VAL*.)* By the way, neither beggar nor borrower be, don't take wooden nickels, why can't we all just get along; Native Americans are no longer angry because we gave them gambling, and homosexuality is somewhat tolerable although we don't encourage it in our own relatives. Have a good one.

(VAL *nods and moves on, books and beer in hand. He finds his own apartment, a one-room hovel with a lamp and a large chair which is also his bed; he sits, opens a beer and takes out a book. After a moment he looks up, composing a letter in his head which we again hear as a voice over.*)

VAL: *(V O)* My Dear Rudi, Alone here in my room, only a mile from who I am but years from who I was, my thoughts return to you. Like a brush fire scorching the terrain of all recent past, your image is unearthed, a memory laced like coal within the crustration of my head, and I burn it as energy, fuel, profoundly vital sustenance. In the smoke that it creates, you seep back through my pores from whence I poured you out; and I learn that one is never so far from one's life as life would have one think. *(Beat)* If you're around, will you call me? Yours, Val.

(*The next day,* VAL *looks for a job. His first interview is with a man named* RON—*played by actor #5—who sits chain smoking behind a desk and talks quite rapidly.*)

RON: Come on in, have a seat, how are you today?

VAL: Good.

RON: Ron Waggle, president of Waggle Job Services, good to meet you.

VAL: Good to meet you, too.

RON: What's your name, son? I have to know your name if I'm gonna find you a job.

VAL: My name is Val.

RON: Val what, Val Hala?

VAL: Val Jones.

RON: Val Jones, that's a good start, Val Jones. It's nice weather out there today, isn't it, Val Jones?

VAL: Yes.

RON: Is it really or are you just saying that to be polite?

VAL: I'm just saying that.

RON: Be honest, Val, that's what prospective employers wanna hear, they want honesty dripping off of you like honey off a bun, okay—no one wants to hire a bullshitter, don't be a bullshitter, Val Jones.

VAL: The weather stinks.

RON: There you go, I like that, you have to have integrity if you want to make it in this world. Do you have integrity?

VAL: Yes.

RON: Never answer yes to that question, Val Jones. Employers want integrity but they don't want you to boast about it; what they're looking for is subtle integrity. Now, of course, never be subtle at the price of honesty. If someone asks you, are you a great banker? you answer, "I'm not a great banker, sir, but I'm a good banker, a good, honest banker with a fair amount of integrity." That's what they want to hear. Trust me, put it on your resume: "Banker, two years, pretty good, definitely honest." Let 'em guess about the integrity. Are you with me?

VAL: Yes.

RON: Okay, let's talk about you, did you bring a resume?

VAL: Yes.

(VAL *hands* RON *a one-page resume;* RON *takes one look.*)

RON: It says here you played baseball in high school.

VAL: Yes.

RON: Why the hell are you telling me that?

VAL: I though prospective employers might appreciate it.

RON: Prospective employers couldn't care jack-boob about you hitting things with a bat. Get rid of this— *(Making large slashes with a pen; he reads on.)* —You mowed lawns?

VAL: Yes.

RON: That's the only job you've ever had?

VAL: I did it spring, summer and fall for eleven years.

RON: Val Jones, I don't care if you mowed every lawn this side of Lawn City U S A, mowing lawns isn't going to get you a real job in the real world. Prospective employers don't care about lawns, they wanna know if you can type.

VAL: Really?

RON: Can you type, Val Jones?

VAL: I learned a lot by mowing lawns—a fair day's wages for a fair day's work; integrity; discipline—

RON: Can you type?

VAL: No.

(RON tears up VAL's resume)

RON: I like you, kid. My instincts tell me not to, but I do. I like you. I genuinely like what I see, perhaps too much, but I think you're a good kid, maybe because you remind me of myself, only more hopeful, you're a hopeful kid, God knows why but it's charming, charming hope, and I like your nonchalance—is it nonchalance or apathy? —Don't tell me, I like the mystery, it's part of your charm. Either way, here's what I'm gonna do: I'm gonna find you a job. This— *(The resume)* —this is shit, never show this to me again, but *you*, I'm gonna see what I can do. *(Hands him a slip of paper)* Go see this man at three o'clock, tell him you were once an honest lawn mower with a couple blades of integrity and that now you're looking to get on the bus. Got it? —Good— Now get outta here.

VAL: Thank you, Ron—

RON: *Get outta here!*

(VAL *leaves and makes his way to the job interview, where a man named* WINSTON—*actor #3—sits behind another desk. He is a rather creepy man of perhaps 55, who wears wireless spectacles and nibbles on an delightfully long piece of red licorice.*)

WIN: You must be Val.

VAL: I am.

WIN: Ron told me you were coming.

VAL: Oh.

WIN: We like Ron.

VAL: Yes.

WIN: My name is Winston—

(WIN *shakes* VAL's *hand*)

WIN: Licorice?

VAL: No thank you.

WIN: I have a separate piece, we don't have to share this one.

VAL: Oh. Okay.

(WIN *hands* VAL *another endless piece of licorice.*)

WIN: So, Val, what did Ron tell you about this job?

VAL: Not very much.

WIN: This is fine licorice, isn't it?

VAL: Yes, it's very good.

WIN: Val, what I have in mind for you is potentially very interesting, but first I'd like to ask you a couple of questions.

VAL: Certainly.

WIN: Val, what would you do if you found a lump of sugar and discovered that it was laced with anthrax?

VAL: I would tell the authorities.

WIN: Which authorities?

VAL: The anthrax authorities.

(WIN *proceeds to write in his notebook for 10 to 20 seconds, then looks up.*)

WIN: Good. Val, if you were given the opportunity to put an anthrax-laced lump of sugar into Adolph Hitler's coffee, *would* you?

VAL: Did Hitler *drink* coffee?

WIN: Assume he did.

VAL: *(Thinks for a moment)* Yes. I would.

(WIN *again writes for an exceedingly long amount of time.*)

WIN: Good. Val, do you think that surrogate mothers for single parents should be paid as much as surrogate mothers for couples?

VAL: Is that really necessary for this job?

WIN: Please just answer the question.

VAL: Yes.

WIN: Val, do you love your mother?

VAL: Yes.

WIN: If given the opportunity, would you sleep with her?

VAL: Absolutely not.

WIN: Why not?

VAL: It would be immoral!

WIN: Says who?

VAL: My mother.

WIN: Let's try this: If you could sleep with anyone in the world—*right now*—with whom would it be?

VAL: Umm...Dolly Parton?

WIN: Superb. Final question: Let's say you were washing a window from the outside, and as you wiped away the dirt, you were able to see inside, and let's say that what you saw was Gandhi meticulously lacing a cube of sugar with an easily lethal amount of anthrax. Would you tell the authorities?

VAL: Without knowing why he was doing it?

WIN: Exactly, with no idea as to what Mohandas was up to.

VAL: I guess I would probably trust his judgment.

WIN: I'd like to hire you, Val, starting tomorrow.

VAL: What's the job?

WIN: Window washer. I think you'll be great at it... there's a certain transparency to you. Be here at nine A M.

(VAL *and* WIN *shake hands and* VAL *is gone, making his way back to his apartment, a sprightly, though somewhat confused stride to his gait......suddenly he is called by* NEW *and* PRO, *his old high school friends.*)

NEW: Hey, Val!

VAL: *(Excited to see them)* Hey New! Hey Pro!

PRO: Actually, I changed my name.

VAL: Oh really—to what?

PRO: Great......Society.

VAL: Cool.

PRO: "If I am for myself alone, then what am I?" Remember that?

VAL: I do.

NEW: And I'm no longer New for New Deal.

VAL: What are you New for?

NEW: Frontier.

VAL: Oh.

PRO: It's time to make the world a better place.

VAL: *(Pause; with admiration)* You always sneak up on me, Pro.

PRO: Great.

VAL: Great.

NEW: So how was your first year of college?

VAL: I'm not going back.

NEW: What?!

PRO: Why not?

VAL: They were teaching me only what *they* wanted me to know. They taught me original thinkers in unoriginal ways. And if I ever had my *own* original thought, I was made to feel like an outsider.

NEW: *(Skeptical)* What was your original thought, Val?

VAL: *(Pause)* I had this idea that I would live my life according to my heart.

NEW: And they didn't go for it?

VAL: They convinced me it was impossible.

PRO: Well they're right. Grow up, Val. This is the world, not a Hallmark card. The heart is a dream we're lucky just to have.

VAL: *(Beat)* Maybe you're right.

NEW: You should really go back.

VAL: *(He is lost in thought.)* Hey, have you guys seen Rudi around?

(NEW *and* PRO *suppress a chuckle or two.*)

NEW: Yeah, we saw Rudi.

VAL: How was she?

NEW: "She" thought she was doing fine.

PRO: You still thinking about her?

(VAL *looks at the ground, shrugs.*)

NEW: We'll see you later, Val.

PRO: Yeah, and stop trying so hard to figure everything out.

(NEW *and* PRO *exit.* VAL *goes home, sits on his bed, opens a book; After a moment,* RUDI *enters, knocking quietly on his door. By all appearances,* RUDI *is now a boy. He is very simply dressed, for there is nothing flashy about this transference. He is simply a boy.*)

VAL: Rudi?

RUDI: Hi, Val.

VAL: It's you?

RUDI: Yeah.

VAL: What......

(RUDI *just looks at* VAL.)

VAL: What happened?

RUDI: How do you mean?

VAL: You seem different.

RUDI: I am.

VAL: How...

RUDI: What?

VAL: How different are you?

RUDI: I'm a boy.

VAL: Why?

RUDI: I was tired of being a girl.

VAL: Did you have a.....

RUDI: Operation?

VAL: Yeah.

RUDI: No.

VAL: But then…?

(Gently, RUDI takes VAL's hand and holds it against his crotch for a moment.)

VAL: *(Simple)* You are. *(Beat)* How?

RUDI: *(With a shrug)* It just happened.

(Pause)

VAL: Did you receive my poem?

RUDI: It was a letter.

VAL: It was a poem.

RUDI: It was nice.

VAL: I'm quitting college.

RUDI: Why?

VAL: I don't know. I guess I'd like to be more original.

(RUDI nods.)

VAL: I like the way you look.

RUDI: Thanks. You too.

VAL: Thanks. *(Beat; ruthlessly earnest)* I don't believe in love anymore.

RUDI: Why not?

VAL: It's just a good idea that never gets off the page.

RUDI: I don't believe in it either.

VAL: Does your adjustment have to do with me?

RUDI: *(Smiles)* Most boys are jerks in high school. You just happened to be the one for me. But there were lots of reasons.

(VAL nods.)

VAL: What do you do these days?

RUDI: I was working as a phone operator for awhile.

VAL: Oh yeah?

RUDI: Yeah. But I got laid off.

VAL: Because of the adjustment?

RUDI: Computer.

VAL: It's supposed to give us more time to think about the big things.

RUDI: I don't believe in the big things anymore.

VAL: *(Nods)* What else do you do?

RUDI: Dance.

VAL: Really?

RUDI: Do you have any music?

VAL: Sure.

(VAL rummages through some junk and pulls out an old cassette player, finds an old cassette.)

VAL: I don't know if you can dance to this.

RUDI: I can dance to anything.

(VAL places a tape in the machine, presses play: Buck Naked by David Byrne, off of David Byrne, and as it plays, VAL and RUDI dance. At first it is just RUDI, moving slowly and to her own beat, and then VAL joins her. Together they now sway, slowly off-rhythm, to the odd and shimmering music.......as a plank of wood descends onto the stage.)

Scene 4

(On the plank of wood sits an OLD WINDOW WASHER *[O W W] —played by actor #5. With a window-washing tool in his hand, he silently and steadily wipes the imaginary window before him. Next to him now is* VAL, *also with washing tool. In* VAL's *other hand is a copy of Moby Dick, from which he reads as he works, his work lacking the industriousness of* O W W's. O W W *seems amused by* VAL's *relaxed attitude. Beat)*

O W W: You're new?

VAL: First day.

O W W: Forty-third year.

VAL: Wow.

O W W: Lotta of soot, grime, filth—but I love it. I'm a fighter. The filth of Satan versus the soap-tears of God.

*(*VAL *extends his hand.)*

VAL: My name is Val.

O W W: *(Shaking his hand)* Ishmael.

VAL: Really?

O W W: That is what they call me.

*(*VAL *excitedly holds up his book.)*

VAL: I've been reading this.

O W W: Why?

VAL: Because it's a classic. The human attempt to flout God, only to be finally delivered to Him in the gaping belly of the great white whale. You see, man has this incessant urge to know if he is alone in the world.

O W W: Uh huh.

VAL: "Once one said God when one looked upon distant seas, but now I have taught you to say otherwise." *(Proudly)* Nietzsche.

O W W: Sometimes it's hard to find God through the soot—

VAL: It's impossible.

O W W: ...the grime, the filth.

VAL: There's so much of it that it belies God's existence!

O W W: Either that or window washing is a dying art.

VAL: *(Slightly smug)* You're trying to teach me a lesson, aren't you?

O W W: No, no—

VAL: Yes you are; you're a wise man.

O W W: I'm just an *old* man washing windows.

VAL: You think young people don't know how to find God anymore; you think our arrogance leads us to believe we can slay the great white whale with our own bare hands.

O W W: My family didn't read that book.

VAL: So then who are you named for?

O W W: Son of Abraham. *This* close to being sacrificed up on the peak of Mount Moriah.

VAL: That was *Isaac*.

O W W: Seven hundred million Muslims think it was Ishmael.

VAL: What's the difference?

O W W: One fathered the Jews, one fathered the Arabs.

VAL: What's your point?

O W W: Point is, *all* fathers sacrifice their sons. They think that's what they're supposed to do. They love 'em so hard, they love 'em to death.

VAL: Are you some kind of religious freak?

(Pause; then, in a quick and sudden motion, O W W *grabs* VAL *by the back of the neck and pushes him forward, threatening to throw him off the edge of the plank)*

O W W: Actually, son, I'm not particularly religious one way or the other, I just like the idea of faith.

VAL: *(Scared)* Faith in what!?

O W W: We'll call it faith in window washing. Doesn't matter what you see so long as there's a clear view; 'cause up here on the peak, it's all about clarity.

VAL: *(Desperate)* I'll wash the window!

O W W: Will you?

VAL: I swear!

O W W: Why?

VAL: Because I believe!

O W W: In what?

VAL: God?!

O W W: Not what I'm looking for.

VAL: Love!?

O W W: Not what I'm looking for.

VAL: Herman Melville!?

*(*O W W *thrusts* VAL *out over the edge even further)*—

VAL: What?! what should I believe in?!

O W W: Not what *should* you believe in?

VAL: What *do* I?

O W W: There you go.

VAL: What *do* I believe in?!

O W W: You tell me.

*(*VAL *is practically dangling from the plank,* O W W *more than content to let him fall.)*

VAL: I don't know.

O W W: *(Another inch closer to the edge)* You better think quick.

VAL: Myself?

O W W: What?

VAL: Please don't kill me—

O W W: What did you say?

VAL: Faith in myself?

O W W: That sounds pretty corny, Val.

VAL: I know.

O W W: I'm up here about to sacrifice you and you're talking about believing in your*self*?

VAL: I agree, it's corny.

(O W W loosens his grip on VAL.)

O W W: But I like it.

(VAL attempts to regain his composure.)

O W W: Don't spend your life quoting old white males. It's a bigger world than that. Figure it out for yourself. *(Pause)* Now let's get back to work.

(VAL returns to work, this time without the book, as the scaffolding rises up and away...)

(SAL and RITA set the table for dinner. They set four places.)

SAL: It doesn't seem right to me.

RITA: He's twenty years old. He can do anything he wants.

SAL: Anything except dropping out of college and dating a hermaphrodite!

RITA: He's a very nice boy. Now.

SAL: I mean—I'm adjusted, I'm all for your low-key homosexuality in certain neighborhoods of east and west coast cities, I even find them to be funkadelic dressers. But when to comes to our son hanging around with a sex-hungry she-male then I have to draw the line!

(VAL *and* RUDI *enter, carrying flowers and a bottle of wine.*)

RITA: Hi there kids!

VAL: Mom, Dad—you guys remember Rudi.

RITA: Of course we do. Hello there, Rudi.

SAL: Bonjourno.

RUDI: Hello.

(VAL *gives* RITA *a kiss and offers her the flowers;* RUDI *offers* SAL *the bottle of wine.*)

RITA: You kids didn't have to do that.

VAL: Oh okay, we'll take it back—

(VAL *jokingly takes the bottle of wine out of* SAL'*s hands as* VAL *and* RITA *laugh too loudly.*)

RITA: Sal, pour some drinks.

(SAL *pours drinks as the others sit.*)

RITA: So, it's good to see you again, Rudi.

RUDI: You too, Mrs Jones.

RITA: Tell me what you've been doing to yourself—*with* yourself since high school?

RUDI: Well, I was working as a phone operator for most of the past year.

SAL: (*Pouring drinks*) At the switchboard?

RUDI: …Yes, actually, but then they came up with a computer program which can do the work of a hundred people.

RITA: Boy oh boy.

(*As* SAL *hands out drinks*)

SAL: Have you been reading the papers, Val?

VAL: I try not to.

SAL: Well you should. Problems in the Marshall Islands.

RUDI: Why?

SAL: They don't like the fact that there's a U S nuclear and intercontinental ballistic missile testing site there.

RITA: That's entirely understandable, Sal.

SAL: Sure, but the problem is, the group that's leading the revolt are radical terrorists who wanna do away with marriage.

RITA: I've never heard of such a thing.

SAL: Well that's what they want and they're determined to fight until all marriage is a thing of the past.

RITA: Well thank God it doesn't have anything to do with us.

SAL: Everything has to do with us, Rita; we're America. *(Point-blank)* Speaking of which: Are you two thinking about marriage?

VAL: *(Pause)* We don't believe in love, Dad.

SAL: Oh we're still playing *that* little game, are we?

VAL: It's not a game—

SAL: *(Intense)* Your mother and I taught you *nothing* if not to love love; we showered you with love from the moment you sprung from this woman's womb, so don't you *dare* sit here and tell me you don't believe in love.

VAL: Fine, we believe in love.

SAL: Don't you *dare* sit here and tell me that you believe in love with this......friend of yours.

VAL: Fine, we don't believe in love.

SAL: So then why're you dating each other?

VAL: We're not.

SAL: So what *are* you doing?!

VAL: Photosynthesis.

SAL: You're photosynthesizing each other?

VAL: Yes, sir.

SAL: *(Quiet—in* VAL's *face:)* Is there *nothing* left of what I taught you that you believe in?

VAL: Such as what?

SAL: To fight for what you believe in.

VAL: I believe in myself, Dad. I wouldn't presume to speak for Rudi.

RUDI: *(With a shy smile)* I believe in myself, too.

*(*VAL *takes his hand and places it in* RUDI's; *very simple:)*

VAL: In fact, I'd go so far as to say that I believe in *us.*

SAL: Don't act more confident than you are, son.

VAL: *(Anger flaring)* Well it just so happens that I *am* confident, Dad. For the first time in my life, I know what I mean, I know what I want and I'm confident in my *self.* And you know what? —If you can't handle that, then you can take an *incredibly* long walk on an *unbelievably* short pier!

SAL: That's it, I'm through with this conversation.

VAL: Why, Dad? Does my being with Rudi go against your sacred "checklist" of stuff I'm supposed to know?

SAL: It goes against everything I taught you!

VAL: You taught me *rhetoric!*

SAL: I taught you *life!*

VAL: *Your* life!

SAL: It was the best I had to give and now you show up acting like a *punk*!

VAL: *(Standing)* Fine then, I'm outta here!

SAL: Fine!

VAL: Fine!!

SAL: *Double frickin' triple* fine!!!!

RITA: Val, don't—

VAL: Forget about it, Mom, it's useless. He's...he's a *Nazi*!!

(Actors freeze as lights alter, flicker, intensify and explode— and VAL *now finds himself the only one alert—desperately looking around for aid, help, succor, love—but everyone else is frozen for several moments...until, one by one, their mouths begin to chant—slow at first but eventually building to an overwhelming rhythm—the following mantras that the now-increasing beating of the drums only serves to accentuate in* VAL's *mind—as the other actors also begin to appear on stage, adorned with the detritus-like threads of our dilapidated pop culture, be it a Chipolte shirt or Google cap or blown-out computer monitor where their head should really be...as their chants gain momentum:)*

SAL: *Fight for what you believe...*

PRO: *"If I am for myself alone, then what am I?"...*

RITA: *Remember, Val, LOVE....*

NEW: *Have faith in yourSELF.... What's up, True Value?...*

SEBUM: *This too shall pass.... Act on your convictions...*

RUDI: *I can dance to anything.*

(The mantras repeat and become louder and louder as VAL, *frenzied, still enraged by* SAL, *loses his mind with increasing speed and fury—gyrating to the now-frenzied drum beat so that he is soon in another dimension, leaving the world, behind, lost,, unchained, insane— ....until quite suddenly*

all sound stops—and VAL, *too, is frozen like the loneliest rock on earth. Blackout)*

(Breath…)

(…when the lights come on, VAL *and* RUDI *are standing quite still, hands held, facing out. On either side of them are* NEW *and* PRO. *Silence for several long moments…… And then—they all speak in rapid fire)*

NEW: Okay then, here it is: The Islanders took over our missile range. They refuse to give it up.

RUDI: I don't blame them.

NEW: I wouldn't either, except for the fact that they're terrorists who subjugate their own people. No marriage, no premarital sex—

PRO: —and plenty of atrocious atrocities.

RUDI: Such as?

PRO: Forced cliterectomies, non-voluntary circumcisions—

VAL: Ow.

RUDI: Maybe that's just the way their culture works.

NEW: Not to be a *dick*, Rudi, but if you'd gone to college you'd know that cultural relativity arguments only go so far. A non-voluntary circumcision is *pure evil*.

RUDI: So is speaking in platitudes.

NEW: *THAT IS SIMPLY NOT TRUE!*

VAL: If they're so evil, why don't we just invade?

PRO: Don't you know who's backing them up? Check it out: Bin Laden, Zarquairi, Adolph Coors, the guy who owns Domino's, Noriega, North Korea, the Serbian National Swim Team, The Third Reich, Idi Amin's cousin, Rupert Murdoch—*AND*—check it out: A very bitter Mario Lopez.

VAL: Damn.

NEW: That's what I'm saying.

PRO: They're already calling it "The Love War".

RUDI: Sounds creepy.

PRO: What're you talking about!? They're ripping out girl's vaginas, sister-man! Cutting off the tips of your little bo-peep! They had a picture in the paper of a big pile of penis tips stacked all the way to the ceiling. Now *that's* creepy.

NEW: It's true, they also showed a man wearing a clitoris necklace.

VAL: Ow.

NEW: That's what I'm saying! But the worst is the law against marriage. Just imagine you couldn't marry the person that you loved!

(The others leave as VAL *and* RUDI *regard one another.)*

VAL: *(To* RUDI*)* Maybe they're right; maybe I *should* fight.

RUDI: You'd *murder* someone?—in the name of *love?*

*(*VAL *turns to the* O W W*, who has suddenly appeared, as* RUDI *exits.)*

O W W: I take it you heard: We're at war.

VAL: Really?

O W W: Declared it ten minutes ago. The United States versus The United Front People's Party of the Marshall Islands...And Friends.

VAL: Do you think I should fight?

O W W: Do you believe in love?

VAL: I've actually been having grave and sincere doubts.

O W W: Do you still wake up each morning?

VAL: Of course.

O W W: Then you probably do.

VAL: I'll wait to see if they institute a draft.

(SAL *enters.*)

SAL: There you have it—they've just instituted a draft!

VAL: When?

SAL: Five minutes ago.

VAL: I thought you weren't talking to me anymore.

SAL: I just wanna make sure you're registered.

VAL: I am.

SAL: (*Suddenly intimate*) Good. Because I know you believe in love, Val. I can see it in your eyes. And even though I don't approve of *who* you love, I love the fact that you do...and that you're willing to fight for it. *To fight for what you believe.* It's what I've always taught you. You do love her, don't you, son?

VAL: *Him.* Yes, Dad. I do.

SAL: Then you should marry...*him.* And you should fight to protect that right.

(*A Black Nazi named* KIRBY, *enters—played by actor #5*)

KIRB: I ain't got nothing against no Marshall Islanders.

VAL: What?

SAL: What?

(VAL *looks from* SAL *to* KIRB, *realizing* SAL *can't perceive* KIRB.)

VAL: (*To* SAL) Nothing.

KIRB: I mean, why should I fight a war ten-thousand miles away when Black people in my own hometown of Reckling*hausen* get treated like shit?

VAL: I guess you have a point.

SAL: I know I do, son.

KIRB: *(In* VAL's *ear)* If the U S is such a noble goddamned democracy, where are they when it *really* counts?

VAL: *(Timid)* Dad, I was wondering why the Allies didn't bomb the train tracks to Auschwitz.

SAL: The G I Bill saved your ass, young man!

KIRB: For me it was the Stuttgart Ballet.

VAL: *(To* KIRB*)* Really?

KIRB: Yeah—just up the road from *Nur-Em-Burg.*

VAL: *(To* SAL*)* What about Nuremburg, Dad?

SAL: What about it?

VAL: *(Not sure at first)* Wasn't the lesson learned there that it's no longer credible to say you were "just following orders"?

SAL: The lesson of Nuremburg was that the world will never again sit back and let genocidal maniacs run wild. If we hadn't stopped Hitler, we'd be standing in the United States of HitlerLand right now. Sometimes people have to die, Val.

KIRB: *(Exiting) Gesundeit, bitch!*

VAL: *Why* do people have to die, Dad?

SAL: Because as you seem to have already figured out, there *is* no God! *(Pause)* I didn't want to tell you when you were younger but maybe I should have. And the fact is, He died a long time *before* Auschwitz, meaning the only thing left now is survival of the fittest. *That's* why you have to fight for what you believe. And if you're not willing to, then maybe you *don't* believe. Maybe that look in your eye when you talk about Rudi is just a pile of horse crap, but I have a feeling it isn't. I have a feeling you believe.

VAL: *(Confused)* In what?

SAL: In *something!* In anything besides nothing. In value, in love, in what's left of this world after God. Anything, Val, just don't give into apathy. *(Urgent)* Do you believe, Val?

(SAL *exits as* RUDI *enters.*)

RUDI: They're detaining me.

VAL: What?

RUDI: The government. I have to go to live in a detention center in Montana.

VAL: Why?

RUDI: They say I'm a threat. That due to the fact of my change—that because of my change, I pose a threat to the security of all Americans. I have to sign a loyalty oath stating I believe in marriage and then I have to live in the camp until the war is over. They said I wasn't "the marrying type".

VAL: Well if you're not then I'm not!

RUDI: But you are, Val. You're the perfect all-American. They love people like you.

VAL: Well in that case I want to marry *you!*

RUDI: *(Quiet)* I thought we said we weren't in love.

VAL: I don't know what else it *can* be!

RUDI: Don't say that—

VAL: I *have* to—

RUDI: Why?

VAL: Because I love you. I know I said I didn't but I do. Even if love *doesn't* exist, I love you. If the heart is just some wet clothes drying in the sun, then those clothes belong to me, because I can't imagine a wardrobe that wouldn't include you. I can't imagine being naked without you by my side; I can't conceive of a day where the image of your smile isn't pasted across my eyelids so that all I have to do is close them and there you are. Because you have conviction, Rudi, like you're on some strange mission to bring integrity to the world. And I've never met anyone like that, who explodes with self-knowledge like a task force from above. I may know nothing about love but I know that you're the one for me, through thick and thin, death and taxes, guns and lawyers, love and hate—you're the reason I wake up, Rudi. I love you so much…. *(Pause)* I'm sorry, but that's all there is to say.

(VAL *and* RUDI *regard one another; after a moment,* MOTHER TERESA, *dressed in casual Nazi garb—played by actor #6—enters. Only* VAL *sees her as she hands him an envelope.)*

VAL: Why do you people keep bothering me?!

RUDI: *(Startled)* What?

VAL: *(To* RUDI*)* Nothing.

RUDI: What is it?

VAL: *(Reading)* My draft notice. I'm to report for my physical in ten days. *(With a sudden vehemence; to* TERESA*)* Why're you doing this to me?!

TERESA: It's your duty.

VAL: To whom?!?

TERESA: Mankind.

RUDI: Val?

VAL: What?!

TERESA: And your *self.*

RUDI: Are you okay?

VAL: No.

(SAL *enters.)*

SAL: My advice to you is to get a haircut *before* you report. You have a much better chance of finding a good civilian barber who'll add a little style while still maintaining the essential crew of the cut.

VAL: Dad, they're sending Rudi to a concentration camp.

SAL: I don't think that's the term you mean to use—

VAL: It is, it's a concentration camp for people who don't fit their description of love.

SAL: She'll be here when you get back.

VAL: What if I *don't* come back?!

(RITA *enters.*)

RITA: You shouldn't say such things, Val.

SAL: Of course he should, if he's not ready to die then he won't make a good soldier.

VAL: Mom?

RITA: Love your motherland, Val.

VAL: But what if you don't agree with it?

RITA: *(Hand on heart)* Then just remember, *love.*

VAL: But what should I *do?*

TERESA: Sometimes people have to die, Val. Many times the lepers came to me begging to die so as to relieve the awful suffering of their loved ones. Willing to sacrifice their bodies for the sake of others.

SAL: There are people being murdered in their sleep, Val, tortured and beaten, limbs hacked off in the name of "community", body parts used for kindling. Husbands and wives are being separated for life because love is considered evil. If you won't fight for that, if you're not willing to *kill*, then you aren't my son. I will be childless! Do you hear? —*Childless!!*

(The Old Window Washer enters again along with actor #3, dressed as a GOVERNMENT OFFICIAL, who now handcuffs Rudi so as to escort him to the detention camp)

VAL: Why're you doing this, Dad?

SAL: Because it's what we taught you.

RITA: The beliefs we instilled.

SAL: Which will carry you through the dark.

O W W: The danger is apathy…

TERESA: The danger is stillness—

O W W: …and not having faith in the *self*.

SAL: *Fight for what you believe in, Val.*

RITA: Don't betray the *love*.

TERESA: Tune in, drop out, fight on.

VAL: Rudi?

(RUDI doesn't answer)

VAL: Do you love me?

RUDI: I don't want to say it, Val.

VAL: Do you love me?!

RUDI: …Yes.

(VAL kisses RUDI on the lips as the GOVERNMENT OFFICIAL prepares to escort RUDI out)

VAL: What're we going to do?

RUDI: Vectorial and topological geometry.

VAL: …in a curvilinear universe?

RUDI: Be *you*, Val. Like no one else.

(RUDI is escorted out. VAL watches, confused)

(VAL then turns to SAL and speaks with definitiveness.)

VAL: *I'm not fucking going, Dad.*

Scene 5

(VAL *enters a large jail cell. Already there are,* JAKE—*a confident though somewhat hyperactively new age young man with thick, black-rimmed glasses, a scull cap and payos—played by actor #5; and* KARA—*a young woman reading a Bible—played by actor #6. They are at home in their communal cell, for it is their home these days.* VAL *stares out between the bars, hands clenched firmly on the steel. After a moment,* VAL *turns to* JAKE:)

JAKE: What grounds?

VAL: What grounds what?

JAKE: What grounds you objecting on? Religious, conscientious, vegetarian?

VAL: *Vegetarian?*

JAKE: We get a lotta veggie-boys in here.

VAL: Moral grounds. I don't believe in murder. *Freedom cannot be compelled. (Extending his hand)* I'm Val.

JAKE: *(Shaking his hand)* Jake Moshe Buddha al-Shabazz. My parents got their Allah mixed up with their challah.

VAL: Why are *you* here?

JAKE: There were five thousand German conscientious objectors found in Dachau and Buchenwald. These things make a difference.

VAL: What difference did *they* make?

JAKE: History. You see, for me, jail is *better* than college. College meant zero to me. I sat behind a cigarette for four years.

VAL: *(A nod)* I guess I'm trying to live by my convictions.

JAKE: Convictions are tricky. As my father, Schlomo Lipschitz, always used to say: Conviction Schlimiction.

VAL: I'm also trying to have faith in myself.

JAKE: Faith Schmaith. It's a double-edged saber. Then again, as my mother's brother, Malik Mohammed Akbar Brahimi Lincoln Lyles the Third, always said: Purity on earth will ensure salvation for eternity. *(Pause)* Then of course you could be like Kara over there. Jehovah's Witness.

(VAL and JAKE both look at KARA, who does not look up from her bible.)

JAKE: Can't wait to rebuild the temple.

VAL: But don't you see? —Religion is all the same. Father figures shoving platitudes down our throats! Leading us to war in the name of some "belief".

JAKE: That's why, in the end, I usually just follow the path of my Mom. Last time I saw her she was wearing her favorite sangha robe, cooking gefilte sandwiches for the annual T N T hajj live-feed from Mecca. I looked at her standing there and I realized what she was. She was everything and nothing, an ongoing revelation, an amalgamation of this world. Her life is living proof that nothing in the world is set in stone.

(Sound of a prison door being opened, followed by the entrance of RHEUM—actor #3—VAL's high school teacher)

RHEUM: Is that you, Val?

VAL: *(Looking up)* Mr Rheum?

RHEUM: Val Jones, my all-time favorite salutatorian of General Schwarzkopf High.

VAL: Mr Rheum, what are you doing here?

RHEUM: It's a long story.

VAL: Are you a conscientious objector also?

RHEUM: Not exactly, but I requested this cell. I like to hang around passive people. Must be the teacher in me.

VAL: *(Introductions)* This is Jake, he's a Jewish Muslim Buddhist who believes that nothing is set in stone, and this is Kara, she's a Jehova's Witness but she's very nice.

RHEUM: Nice to meet you both. *(Looking around)* So, this is home for the next seventeen years.

VAL: Seventeen years? What on earth did you do?

RHEUM: Oh, it's a long story…stupid, archaic laws meant only to curtail human freedom. What about you?

VAL: I took a stand against the Love War.

RHEUM: Why?

VAL: Because how can one *fight* for *love*? It doesn't make sense.

RHEUM: Nothing makes sense, Val, didn't they teach you that in college?

VAL: They did, but I dropped out because I felt that things *did* make sense, even if I didn't know what they were.

RHEUM: I see.

VAL: Come to think of it, Mr Rheum, you were the first one to teach me that; that not everything my parents told me was to be believed.

RHEUM: And you believed that?

VAL: *(Momentarily thrown off)* Yes. The fact is, I very much admire the life path you've chosen for yourself, Mr Rheum. You offer an alternative to the standard belief systems. *(Beat)* Mr Rheum, why're you in jail?

RHEUM: A silly rule about not sleeping with one's students.

VAL: …You slept with a student?

RHEUM: I'm afraid it was more than one.

VAL: How many?

RHEUM: Two hundred and thirteen. But over a twelve year period.

VAL: That's more than seventeen students a year!

RHEUM: You always were good at math, Val.

VAL: How could you do that?!

RHEUM: Logistically, it was often tricky. And of course it wasn't always an even average, some years there were as many as thirty-five. One has only so many free periods per day.

VAL: I looked up to you, Mr Rheum!

RHEUM: Did you? I don't remember your face from that angle.

VAL: ……Was there ever anyone from my class?

RHEUM: Let me think…well, of course there was Rudi—

VAL: *(Broken)* Rudi?

RHEUM: Determined young girl, full of integrity. Although in light of what she became, I'm not so sure I don't regret it…

VAL: *(Suddenly violent)* I should kill you!

RHEUM: Don't be mad, Val, I just never found you that enticing. Granted, you're more attractive now. You seem to have grown into yourself—

VAL: I *love* Rudi!!

RHEUM: And she loved you. She told me so repeatedly. Her taste for me was just a small time crush, a father figure handing out the grades.

(The Beatles' All You Need Is Love *begins a slow build, as* VAL *internally processes a swelling internal violence…)*

VAL: *(To self, determined)* Okay, Dad—you want me to fight for what I believe?…

*(*VAL *now approaches* RHEUM *and shoves him in the chest,)*

VAL: I'm gonna kill you—

RHEUM: Thou shalt not kill, Val—

VAL: *(Shoving again)* I'm going to fucking kill you—

RHEUM: Try to get over it.

VAL: Why?!

RHEUM: Because this too shall pass.

VAL: No it won't—

RHEUM: Believe me—

VAL: Stop talking—

RHEUM: Val, don't be silly—

VAL: Shut the hell up—

RHEUM: Val!—

*(*VAL *now has* RHEUM *up against the wall)*—

RHEUM: She wanted it, you have to accept that!—

*(*VAL *violently knees him in the groin;* RHEUM *doubles over,* VAL *grabs him around the neck and starts choking,* RHEUM *is defenseless. The music increasing in volume, as* JAKE *yells for* VAL *to stop, though his pacifist leanings forbid him from jumping in; and* KARA *watches, her Bible resting calmly on her lap. Every ounce of* VAL's *energy and focus are committed to his intent—the death of* RHEUM—*as the music intensifies and* RHEUM *gasps, then sputters……and then is still: As* VAL *freezes—)*

(—*and we realize, along with,* VAL *[who realizes subliminally], that a battle is taking place in a far off land. We are watching* NEW *and* PRO *desperately fight for their lives from a foxhole; they are continually bombarded and shot at. Repeatedly, they stick their heads and guns out of the foxhole to fire at the unseen enemy, only to duck back in for cover from the intense fire they are receiving. Suddenly,* PRO *leaps up and out of the foxhole and stands alone, screaming and firing her gun in slow motion—)*

PRO: C'MON YOU FUCKING PRICK-FUCKS, I'LL FUCKING KILL EVERY LAST ONE OF YOU, YOU TERRORIST NON-LOVE-LOVING MOTHERFUCKERS!!!

(PRO *continues to fire and scream like a mad woman,* NEW *desperately scurries out of the foxhole and attempts to pull her back in, but she remains defiant—shooting and screaming, screaming and shooting with a primal urgency. The scene is drawn out, horrific, brutal, elegiac, as* NEW *tries to wrestle her back into the foxhole…but his strength is muted by her will…… * VAL *may or may not be literally watching all this, but he is, without a doubt, feeling it on an intensely guttural level…….as* PRO *now dies a slow, painful death in* NEW's *arms. Music and lights shift—back to* VAL, *knee atop the now-dead* RHEUM. *In a desperate and sudden motion,* VAL *raises his head to the heavens and screams out at the top of his lungs:)*

VAL: *SHRINNNKKKK!!!!*

(VAL *is immediately seated with a prison psychiatrist,* DR BYSMA—*played by actor #1)*

BYSMA: Would you like to tell me why you killed your high school English teacher?

VAL: You remind me of my mother.

BYSMA: Use it. *(Pause)* You do realize that your prison sentence has now been extended to twenty-three years?

VAL: *(Quiet; almost to himself)* I acted on my convictions; and I was convicted. I fought for what I believed in. And I became a murderer. I remembered to love, *always*. And I filled with hate. I had faith in my *self*. *(Even quieter)* And now I don't. *(Pause; he looks up)* What kind of shrink are you?

BYSMA: I do Freudian, Jungian, rolfing, Gestalt, heller, healing, hypnosis, rebirthing, re-channeling and a sorta hybrid form of astrology-meets-SnapChat.

VAL: *(Pause)* There are Nazis in my life. Friendly ones.

BYSMA: …Do they speak to you?

VAL: Sometimes. I also never masturbate.

BYSMA: You should.

VAL: Really?

BYSMA: A lot. Have you ever had any *real*-life association with Nazis?

VAL: No.

BYSMA: Do you have a personal definition of evil?

VAL: Nazis.

BYSMA: Why?

VAL: Because they murdered people.

BYSMA: *You* just murdered somebody.

VAL: But he was guilty.

BYSMA: Of what?

VAL: I feel like I'm being psychoanalyzed.

BYSMA: Val—why do you think the notion of a friendly Nazi has found its way into your subconscious?

VAL: I would like to leave now.

BYSMA: I'm afraid you can't—

VAL: Fuck you I wanna leave—

BYSMA: Why?

VAL: Because I'm evil—

BYSMA: You're not evil, Val—

VAL: Fuck you, I'm evil and I'm tired of you and I'm
tired of definitions! Definitions don't exist. *Nothing*
exists. Existence is just a bunch of nameless kids
hacking each other to death as we watch on T V with
the sound turned down pretending to read a book
by some dead plagiarist who lives in Switzerland
and consistently beats his wife! You know what I'm
saying!? Latin's a dead language, Shakespeare wasn't
Shakespeare, morality's a strip of turkey bacon and
computers are made of quarks strung together like
clitorises on a necklace choking my neck which doesn't
even exist! And you know what else?!—I'm outta here!

(VAL *collapses in a heap;* BYSMA *stands over him and speaks
gently*)

BYSMA: My initial diagnoses, Val, is that you have
"*issues.*" In the process of reconsidering your life, you
have been confronted with a number of new notions:
friendly Nazis, your mentor screwing your lover, your
lover having a penis, the idea that right and wrong,
good and evil, true and false—don't mean what you
thought they did. A friendly Nazi is a heretofore
unconsidered notion, and its contemplation has left
you bereft of any hierarchal understanding of the
world. For all your efforts, you've actually ended up
transparent.

(VAL *pivots…and is back in his cell.*)

JAKE: Yo, my brother, the war's over.

VAL: The war's over?

JAKE: That's what I said.

VAL: Who won?

JAKE: We did. Sort of. The testing site is still under our control but we gave all the Islanders who work there full coverage for pre-existing conditions. Plus we forced them all to marry each other.

VAL: *Everybody* got married?

JAKE: Yeah. Except for the ones who got killed. Big wedding. Flew in Reverend Moon.

VAL: How many died?

JAKE: Twenty thousand Marshall Islanders and one American. Some girl named Great Society.

(*Beat;* VAL *silently begins to cry. Watching this,* KARA *stands, walks through the prison bars to him and lightly touches his shoulder; she is a gentle person.*)

KARA: Be strong.

VAL: (*Through silent tears*) Why?

KARA: Because it's all part of a plan. "In thy darkest hour, there will be light, for though man is born to trouble, the sparks fly upward."

(VAL *looks up at* KARA.)

KARA: Your teacher's behavior was a sign; so was your killing him. Pestilence, plagues, murder.

VAL: I'm not a religious person.

KARA: "Religion is what you find when you're alone."

VAL: (*Weak*) I wouldn't even know what to believe *in*.

KARA: (*Placing Bible in his lap; simple*) If you build it, He *will* come.

(KARA *leaves* VAL *to ponder this...and suddenly he is back with a* DRAFT OFFICER—*played by actor #2. The "*D O*," a cheerful man—more playful than mean.*)

D O: To be honest, Val, there *is* some sympathy on the Committee apropos your case. The "Deadly

Conscientious Objector, compelled to kill by the claustrophobia of his confinement." There's a chance they'll find some leniency in their hearts.

VAL: That's good.

D O: We're a good country. There's something very American in being American.

VAL: In God we trust.

D O: Exactly. And of course, now that you've found religion, the committee's inclined to offer you the new option.

VAL: New option?

D O: Freedom for a Foot Program. Nifty little idea we lifted from the Islanders.

VAL: What's Freedom for a Foot?

D O: Means we chop off one of your toes for every five years we reduce your sentence. Thus for you, freedom is four and a half toes.

(D O *reaches behind his desk and produces an enormous double-edged saber; Val looks scared*)

VAL: Would I get Novocain?

D O: No pain, no gain, Val.

VAL: ...Okay.

D O: *Great!* Choose a foot and de-shoe yourself!

(VAL *nervously takes off his shoe;* D O *then lays* VAL's *foot out before him and attempts to line up the saber.* VAL *is scared but determined, sort of.* D O *lifts the saber above his head*)

D O: You're a tough little pacifist.

VAL: Thanks.

D O: Ready?

VAL: I think.

D O: Good.

(VAL *nods;* D O *lifts the saber even higher above his head…..then slams it down across* VAL's *toes, as lights radically shift—)*

Scene 6

(VAL's *childhood home.* RITA *is alone in the kitchen, making herself an elegant-appearing dinner. She listens to music— early James Brown as she works. After several moments,* VAL *enters, carrying his bag and limping somewhat noticeably. He watches his mother dance. She is quite obviously younger, her vernacular, dress and mannerism reflecting a heretofore unseen contemporary flavor, although she retains a certain wisdom…. None of this is lost on him, as he watches her cook and dance…..)*

VAL: Mom?

(RITA *looks up.)*

RITA: Val?!

VAL: Mom?

RITA: *They let you out?!*

(VAL *nods.* RITA *runs to him and they embrace, each one close to tears.)*

RITA: I can't believe it! Are you okay? They didn't hurt you, did they?

VAL: No, Mom.

RITA: Oh, Val, it's so wonderful!

VAL: Mom? You're different.

RITA: The war was hard on all of us, child.

VAL: You seem younger.

RITA: Hmmmm hmmm.

VAL: And you're really…beautiful.

RITA: Ain't I a woman?

VAL: Where's Dad?

RITA: Val, your Daddy moved out.

VAL: What?! …*Why*?

RITA: Separate directions. Like you say—I'm different.

VAL: But just like that? After twenty-five years?

RITA: When else?

VAL: But—

RITA: Things happen, Val. You should know that by now.

(VAL *absorbs.*)

VAL: Is it all right if I stay here for awhile? Until I get back on my feet?

RITA: Sure 'nuff, Poopy.

(VAL *puts down his suitcase, confused by his "new" Mom.*)

VAL: I have to go find Rudi. (*Stopping at the door*) I love you, Mom.

RITA: Back at you, Poopy.

VAL: Can you please stop calling me Poopy? I mean, what does that even *mean*? Do you actually think I'm poopy?

RITA: It's just a term of affection, mijo.

VAL: No it's not! There's no etymological research showing that "Poopy" is a term of affection!

RITA: I didn't say there was, it's just my own *personal* term. (*Giddy*) I made that shit up! Just this instant! But *fine*, mijo—no more Poopy!

(VAL, *confused, turns and walks determinedly, with his limp, into town. Suddenly an affable, bearded man* [PURE]

—played by actor #3—carrying a bag and dressed in a Nazi bathrobe, calls to him, possibly in a German accent.)

PURE: Excuse me!

VAL: Yes?

PURE: Val?

VAL: Yes.

PURE: *(Extending his hand)* Hi, I'm Pure, I'd like to have a quick word with you, if I may?

VAL: *Pure?*

PURE: Yes.

VAL: Pure what?

PURE: Evil. Pure Evil. It's good to finally meet you.

(VAL and PURE shake.)

PURE: Listen, I hear you're looking for a father figure.

VAL: No.

PURE: I hear you're looking for some direction in your life.

VAL: Even if I was, I would never find either of those from a Nazi.

PURE: How do you know I'm so bad? Maybe I'm not—

VAL: You're *Pure Evil!*

PURE: It's just a *name!* These are merely *clothes!* Look—I can drop 'em both—

(PURE whips off his bathrobe, beneath which he wears a Hilfiger Speedo. He extends his hand.)

PURE: Look—Tommy *HEIL*figer! And guess what?— you can call me Archibald!

(As VAL watches, PURE drops his hand and begins to dance around, singing happily.)

PURE: I'm nakeedd! I'm nakeeeddd! No more Nazi! I'm Buck Naked Archibalddd! *(He stops dancing.)* Hey, did you hear the one about Abraham? *(No answer)* He was an *uber-mensch!* *(He goes into his bag and takes out a large Oscar Award statue, holds it triumphantly above his head.)* I guess this means you like me! You really, really *like* me!!

(Suddenly, PURE hears someone coming, grabs his robe and bag and starts to exit.)

PURE: I'm outta here— *(He stops, turns back.)* —But just remember—no matter how you slice it or dice it— *everybody* looks good naked!

(PURE scurries off as another man appears. He is a BROKEN MAN—played by actor #5—possibly homeless, indubitably joyless, wrapped in a blanket...and mumbling.)

MAN: Nice day, assfuck.

VAL: What?

MAN: Hell in a hand bucket, jack of all trades, right is might, beans and motherfuckers.

(Something about this MAN catches VAL's attention.)

VAL: Excuse me?

MAN: Catholic girls go round and round, Tuskegee fuck, Athens was a dump....

VAL: New? ...Is that you?

(The MAN looks up at VAL. It is, in fact, his old friend NEW, aka New Deal, aka New Frontier)

NEW: Who's that?

VAL: It's me. Val.

NEW: Val?

VAL: Val! From high school.

(NEW *now recognizes* VAL. *He takes him in, then looks away*)

NEW: How are you?

VAL: I'm good. Not bad. How are *you?*

NEW: Better fucking days. *(Pause)* You called me wrong.

VAL: I called you "New".

NEW: It's not my name anymore.

VAL: You changed again?

NEW: Yeah. Bridge. *(Pause)* To the Twenty-first Century.

VAL: Oh.

NEW: *(Fist in air)* Keep hope alive. Yes we can. Not so sure.

VAL: ...What's happened to you, Bridge?

NEW: Tough year. Bridge too far.

(Beat)

VAL: I heard about Pro.

NEW: You mean Great.

VAL: Yeah. Great Society.

NEW: Died in my arms.

VAL: I'm sorry.

NEW: What, that you weren't there with us?

VAL: If I said that, it wouldn't be true.

NEW: What would it be?

VAL: It would be a polite thing to say. *(Pause)* I was fighting for what I believed in.

NEW: No you weren't.

VAL: Well, okay—but, I was acting on my convictions. I think.

NEW: …Free agency's killing baseball. No one's got any loyalty to their team anymore. It's all about the money.

VAL: Yes. It's different.

NEW: It's got nothing to do with America. *(Beat)* But we gave her a nice funeral.

VAL: Great Society?

NEW: Yeah. Nice flowers.

VAL: I'm sorry I wasn't there.

NEW: You were in jail?

VAL: Yeah. *(Beat)* Do you need a place to stay, Bridge?

NEW: No, I'm all right.

VAL: Call me if you do.

NEW: *(He nods; beat)* You're probably looking for Rudi.

(VAL nods.)

NEW: He went back to female.

VAL: Really?

NEW: Working over at the Lolita Lounge on Connie Ave. Calls herself Candy.

VAL: Thanks, Bridge.

NEW: Take it to the bridge.

(As VAL and NEW part ways……)

(……and we are now watching RUDI, dressed as a "sexy woman" performing a provocative poll dance….moments later, the song ends to scattered applause and she returns to her dressing room in a silk robe. As she takes off her wig, she sees VAL. They regard one another.)

RUDI: Hey.

VAL: Hey.

(Beat; VAL and RUDI hug, although it is a tentative embrace. She is not at all how he has remembered her throughout his prison term.)

VAL: It's good to see you.

RUDI: You too.

VAL: How was the detention camp?

RUDI: Bad.

VAL: *(Beat)* What're you doing here, Rudi?

RUDI: This is where I work.

VAL: At a strip club?

RUDI: Yes.

VAL: Why?!

(RUDI does not feel like answering this; VAL softens his approach)

VAL: You're not a boy anymore?

RUDI: None of us are.

VAL: You know what I mean.

RUDI: No—I'm no longer a boy.

VAL: Why not?

RUDI: All I was doing was running away from being a woman.

VAL: And what're you doing now?

RUDI: Running *to* it.

VAL: By selling your body to a bunch of drunk perverts?

RUDI: I make a lot of money, Val. I get to dance. I'm in complete control of everything I do.

VAL: It's sad.

RUDI: Why, because I'm untouchable?

VAL: Because God tells us that our soul will be lost if we succumb to temptations of the flesh.

RUDI: Don't talk like that.

VAL: Like what?

RUDI: Religiously.

VAL: I've offered myself up for salvation.

RUDI: Oh Jesus—

VAL: Why?

RUDI: I can't believe you would go and do that—

VAL: Do what?

RUDI: After everything we went through.

VAL: Look who's talking!—

RUDI: At least I'm not a Jesus freak!

VAL: I'm not a Jesus freak, Rudi! I just figured that if I believe in love, which I *do*, then I should also believe in God, since that's where love comes from.

RUDI: Kum-by-fucking-ya.

VAL: Will you come home with me? *(No answer)* Why not?

RUDI: Because I spent too many years trying to belong to somebody.

VAL: Is that why you slept with Mr Rheum in high school?

(Beat; RUDI *has never before been confronted by this.)*

RUDI: High school was not a happy time. Mr Rheum was an effort to stop the confusion.

VAL: Did it work?

RUDI: Obviously not.

VAL: *(Beat)* Did you love me?

RUDI: A long time ago.

VAL: And now?

RUDI: Now is different. It's no longer photosynthesis, Val.

VAL: What is it?

RUDI: It's oxygen.

(The sounds of King Sunny Ade. RUDI disappears; VAL turns and limps back to his home, where RITA is pouring herself a glass of Merlot. Seeing VAL, she turns the music down.)

RITA: Did you find Rudi?

VAL: Yes.

RUDI: The magic's gone?

VAL: She says it has to do with oxygen.

RITA: *She*?

VAL: Yes.

RITA: Well I *do* give her credit.

VAL: Why?

RITA: Because she knows how to become. Even if she sometimes becomes the wrong thing.

VAL: I don't understand.

RITA: It's about breathing, Val. The reason I seem younger isn't because I'm trying, it's because I'm breathing. And by breathing I become. I let the world pass through me. If I held my breath until your father came back, I'd be dead ten times over. You can't battle life, Val. Sadness is a virtue. It's beauty cream. If applied gently, it can add years to your life.

VAL: *(Sad)* But I went to prison for her.

RITA: You went to prison for yourself.

VAL: But it was because I loved her. *You* were the one who told me to always believe in love.

RITA: Yes. Now love whatever comes next. Love her loss, love your faith, your loss of faith, your violence, your loneliness, your breath…your ability to become.

VAL: Become what?

RITA: Whatever comes next.

VAL: But doesn't that make me nothing?

RITA: Not if you do it with conviction. Not if you *believe* in the act of your becoming.

VAL: I would like to do that.

RITA: Then let go.

VAL: Of—?

RITA: Of everything you thought you knew.

(Beat; VAL is watching RITA.)

RITA: Stop looking at me like I'm an old lady.

VAL: But that's what you're supposed to be.

RITA: I became something else. A heretofore unconsidered notion.

(Beat; VAL and RITA are now very close. With extreme hesitation, he starts to try to kiss her…but at the last moment she gently stops him, her hand on his cheek.)

VAL: But… "The heart wants what the heart wants." Shakespeare.

RITA: No, Val. That was Woody Allen. You need to be more original. No more clichés. *(Pause; intimate)* Act as if you're breathing for the first time.

VAL: But then I won't know what I'm doing.

RITA: Good.…

(VAL closes his eyes…and she disappears. He opens his eyes to the emptiness. Suddenly an OLD MAN—*played by actor #2—enters. He is dressed in what can only be described as pre-Christian garb. He carries a small, double-edged saber.)*

OLD: Excuse me, young man, have you seen my son?

VAL: *(Beat)* Your son?

OLD: Yes. My son.

VAL: What does he look like?

OLD: Timid boy. Wears sandals. Screwed up for life.

VAL: *(Beat)* No.

OLD: Well, if you see him, will you tell him I'm sorry?

VAL: Sorry for what?

OLD: For following orders.

VAL: *(Pause)* Sure.

OLD: Thank you.

*(*OLD *starts to leave.)*

VAL: Is that why he's screwed up for life? Because you were following orders?

OLD: Yes. I was doing what I thought I was supposed to. But in the end, it wasn't about him. It was for myself.

VAL: But weren't you acting on your convictions?

OLD: I was doing it for myself.

VAL: But you believed. In what you were doing. You weren't dishonest.

OLD: Yes. You're right. I believed. *(Pause)* But I imagine he feels betrayed.

VAL: Not if he knows you did it out of love. It was the best gift you had to give; the power of your belief; mistakes and all. Piled high with your shortcomings.

OLD: *(Beat)* Yes, well....

(OLD *pauses, then hands the saber to* VAL.)

OLD: If you see him, you'll give him this? Yes?

VAL: *(Accepting)* Sure.

OLD: Thank you. *(Beat)* Good luck to you.

VAL: Yes. You too.

OLD: No, really—good luck. My son.

(OLD *exits.* VAL *watches him go...and then determinedly turns to walk in the other direction, but before he has taken two steps he finds* RUDI *already there.* RUDI *is now neither a boy or a girl. Gone are the silk robe and breasts, as are the indications of masculinity. There is simply* RUDI.)

RUDI: Hello.

VAL: Hello. *(Pause)* I was coming to find you.

RUDI: Why?

VAL: Because I know what to do with the oxygen.

RUDI: What?

VAL: Breathe. To feel each breath. Like for the first time. *(Pause)* All I know is that I love you. And I don't even know that. I just think I do.

RUDI: I think I do too.

VAL: Why?

RUDI: Love *has* no why.

(VAL *now regards* RUDI.)

VAL: You're not a girl.

RUDI: No.

VAL: Are you a boy?

RUDI: I don't think so.

VAL: What are you?

RUDI: I'm breathing.

(VAL *and* RUDI *smile…and breathe together.* RITA *enters, seeming dazed, even devastated.*)

RITA: Val.

VAL: Yes?

RITA: Your father's dead.

(VAL *is stunned.*)

RITA: He checked back into the hospital last night, complaining of chest pains. He suffered a stroke fifteen minutes ago. He's gone.

VAL: He can't be.

RITA: I'm sorry.

VAL: I just talked to him.

RITA: He's been sick for weeks. I should've told you earlier. I thought he'd pull through.

VAL: But he was just here, Mom. He gave me this saber. He said he was sorry.

(RITA *just looks at* VAL. *He realizes she's telling the truth; beat…*)

VAL: Will he have a twenty-one gun salute?

RITA: (*Regarding him almost sympathetically*) Val, your father never fought against the Nazis.

VAL: What're you talking about, Mom? He deserves a proper military burial. He killed two hundred Gestapo.

RITA: No. He spent the war washing windows. They wouldn't let him fight on account of his hearing. Bad ears. (*Pause*) He was never a good listener.

VAL: (*Beat…*) How come he didn't tell me the truth about himself?

RITA: I suppose he wanted to pass on a legacy that you would cherish. (*Beat*) Instead, you got his ears.

VAL: *That's* my legacy? Bad ears?

RITA: No. Your legacy is to listen. To be better. To put your ear to the ground, wait for the earth to grumble, then figure out how to act.

VAL: *(Beat)* I didn't even say goodbye.

RITA: That's usually how it works.

(RUDI *comforts* VAL.)

VAL: What do we do now?

RITA: We go to the hospital. Claim the body.

VAL: Claim it?

RITA: Claim it. Claim the man, then bury him.

(The lights have changed and VAL, RUDI *and* RITA *now stand at a modest grave site, holding hands. Other actors enter quietly in the background. A* MAN—*played by actor #2—in a nondescript robe, stands nearby and reads from an unidentified book.)*

MAN:
How calm—how beautiful comes on
That stilly hour, when storms have gone
When warring winds have died away
And clouds, beneath the dancing ray
Melt off and leave the land and sea
Sleeping in bright tranquility

(…as VAL *takes out the double-edged saber and gently rests it on the freshly dug earth….)*

RUDI: *(To* VAL*)* Just breathe.

MAN: *(Cont:)* …and this too, shall pass..…

(Quietly, the song Buck Naked *begins to play again…….as the lights fade to black.….)*

END OF PLAY

GEOMETRY OF FIRE

GEOMETRY OF FIRE was produced Off-Broadway at the Rattlestick Playwrights Theater, opening on 24 November 2008. The cast and creative constributors were as follows:

MEL .... Kevin O'Donnell
TARIQ .... Donnie Keshawarz
BOB, CHUCK .... Jeffrey DeMunn
CYNTHIA, *other women* .... Jennifer Mudge

Director .... Lucie Tiberghien
Set design .... Robin Vest
Costume design .... Anne Kennedy
Lighting design .... Peter West
Sound design .... Broken Chord Collective

CHARACTERS

MEL ANDERSON, *white, very late 20s*
TARIQ "T-BONE" AL-TURKI, *Saudi-American, 30s*
BOB, *white, mid 50s; (same actor plays* CHUCK*)*

female actor—CYNTHIA *and other parts, white, 30s*

(*A dim stage. Light finds* MEL—*a bit unkempt, maybe a beard; an Oxford cutoff, combat boots. He speaks fairly quietly:*)

MEL: I was an economics major. (*Pause*) But I never joined a frat. (*Pause*) I think that's all you need to know. (*He just stands there…*)

(—*as light rises on another part of the stage, where* TARIQ, *a charming, odd guy dressed a bit like a member of the Stray Cats, silently makes love to a woman,* CYNTHIA, *30s, in a cemetery; a headstone helps them to remain mostly upright. She wears a dress that's now hiked up, while his jeans are awkwardly down around his ankles making him look a bit idiotic. They quietly make steady love.*)

MEL: (*To audience*) I'm choosing to ignore that.

(MEL *leaves…as the cemetery sex partners achieve something of a climax and now relax quietly…. After a moment,* CYNTH *and* TAR *begin to slowly get dressed*)

TAR: That was fun.

CYNTH: For the most part.

(TAR *just smiles.*)

CYNTH: I'm assuming you were lying about this graveyard. (*Pause*) About your dad.

TAR: I'm not lying. That's his headstone.

(CYNTH *doesn't believe this…but then she checks the name on it just to be sure; she can't help but look relieved*)

CYNTH: I'm gonna run with the idea that your last name's not Jones.

TAR: If that's what you need.

CYNTH: *(Smile; pause)* Is your Dad really dead?

TAR: Yeah. *(Pause)* No. *(She just looks at him.)* I mean he's three-fourths there. Cancer.

CYNTH: *(Fairly genuine)* Sorry.

TAR: It's been a long time coming, Squaw-girl.

(CYNTH and TAR continue getting dressed)

TAR: So do you like working at that place, Rhoda?

CYNTH: Cynthia.

TAR: Cynthia. *(Pause; he extends his hand)* Hey, Cynthia, I'm T-Bone.

CYNTH: Nice to meet you.

TAR: So…do you—

CYNTH: Do I like being a bartender?

TAR: Yeah.

CYNTH: No.

TAR: I'd never been to that bar. It's nice.

CYNTH: What do *you* do, "T-Bone"?

TAR: Professional fuck up.

(CYNTH just sorta nods.)

TAR: The whole three-fourths dead father thing…

CYNTH: Do you have a Mom?

TAR: Car crash. Many moons ago.

CYNTH: Wow. I'm sorry.

TAR: She was hit by a Ford, so I've come to think of it as patriotic. *(Beat; he sips from a bottle of beer.)* You're really sweet. I mean beautiful. I mean you seem really morally upstanding.

CYNTH: Thank you.

TAR: I've been interviewing women as prospective girlfriends, and if this were one of those interviews, you'd be at the top of my list.

CYNTH: That's funny, 'cause I had you pegged for gay.

TAR: ...There are days that I am.

(TAR *opens one of several Bud Lights he has with him, offering* CYNTH *one as well, which she accepts; beat.*)

CYNTH: So do you have a *lot* of casual sex in graveyards?

TAR: Was that casual?

CYNTH: Maybe not.

TAR: *(Pause)* When I was a kid I used to pretend my parents were buried here. I'd drive by with my dad and just, you know...imagine.

CYNTH: That they were both dead?

TAR: Yeah. *(Pause)* But I've been wanting to come by here recently.

CYNTH: Why?

TAR: I dunno. Maybe because of what this lady told me the other day. *(Pause; deadpan)* This perhaps explains why I succumbed to the irresponsible encounter of a one-night stand.

CYNTH: ...What lady?

TAR: It's this lady who's putting together a lawsuit. Which basically says that the neighborhood where I grew up used to be a chemical weapons testing ground.

(CYNTH *just looks at him, unsure whether he's joking*)

TAR: I'm serious.

CYNTH: No you're not.

TAR: Yeah I am. Google it. *(Pause)* You know about Google?

CYNTH: Yeah.

TAR: Google the fuck out of it.

CYNTH: ...Where did you live?

TAR: Around here. Behind A U. I still do.

CYNTH: There was a chemical weapons testing ground in Washington D C?

TAR: Yeah, during World War One. And there's this whole group of people who live there who think they're getting sick because of it.

CYNTH: Sick like—?

TAR: Like with Multiple Myeloma. Like my dad.

CYNTH: ...Do you think what she said is true?

TAR: Hard to say, I'm a fuck-up.

CYNTH: Right, but if you're a fuck-up, doesn't that mean you have some time on your hands to sort of, check those types of theories out? I mean it's a pretty intense—

TAR: "Allegation"?

CYNTH: *(A small smile)* Yeah.

TAR: *(Pause)* I'm feeling extremely connected to you.

(CYNTH smiles at TAR's stupidity...)

TAR: What's kinda weird is that ever since this lady called, the only happy image I've been able to, like, conjure of my Dad is of him eating this enormous tomato. *(Pause)* He's wearing a really high-end *robe* and eating a tomato from this garden we had out back. *(Pause)* I may be making this up. *(Pause)* But we definitely had a garden. And there was definitely some tomato juice dribbling down my father's cheek.

And he looked totally happy; in his little headdress; with tomato *pulp* on his chin. *(Beat)* Are we becoming intimate with each other?

CYNTH: Do you have a job, T-Bone?

TAR: I run a car service.

CYNTH: Oh.

TAR: Very high end clients.

CYNTH: …Are you serious?

TAR: Not *that* high-end, but… You want my card? It's like a private limo thing. I have those little airline bottles of vodka in the back.

CYNTH: *(Off his card)* It's just you?

TAR: Yeah. Great hours.

(CYNTH just looks at TAR.)

TAR: I'm not one of those guys burdened by ambition.

(CYNTH nods, smiling…pockets the card….)

TAR: Do you go on dates with people, Cynthia? If they ask you?

CYNTH: *(A smile; pause)* What's your *real* name, T-Bone?

TAR: …Tariq.

(A smile…as lights shift—)

(And MEL steps into the "office" of a harried but genuinely concerned Veterans Affairs psychiatrist named WANDA, in civilian clothes— [played by the female actor]. The office is rundown and cluttered, as represented by a run-down and cluttered desk)

WAN: I'm sorry to keep you waiting.

MEL: It's all right.

WAN: How long were you out there?

MEL: An hour.

WAN: *Really?* Oh God I'm sorry. They're just loading me up these days, *loading* me up the wazzoo.

MEL: Well for what it's worth, each guy walked out looking like a million bucks.

WAN: *Really? (No answer)* Right—okay. *So*—sit down and let's talk about *you*.

(MEL *sits, as does* WAN, *who plucks his file from a big pile and looks it over.)*

MEL: They told me I should see the V A guy but you're not really a guy.

WAN: No I'm not. I'm Wanda, the V A *woman*. Hear me roar. *(Looking up)* So. You've been back four months?

MEL: Yeah.

WAN: And according to this you were in good shape upon your return, except for some high blood pressure?

MEL: Yep.

WAN: How's that going for you now?

MEL: No pressure at all.

WAN: *(A smile)* Okay, well let's have a looksy. *(During the following, she checks his blood pressure)* How are you feeling otherwise?

MEL: Fine.

WAN: Is there something specific that brings you in today?

MEL: My dad says I'm chronically detached.

WAN: That's quite a diagnosis.

MEL: He reads *Newsweek*.

WAN: Is he right?

MEL: No.

WAN: Any other symptoms besides the blood pressure?

MEL: Problems sleeping. Some temper stuff.

WAN: Understandable. Anything else?

MEL: I keep wanting to watch William Hurt movies.

WAN: *(A smile, then, re: blood pressure)* Still high. 140 over 90.

MEL: That could be *Body Heat.*

WAN: …Are you drinking more than usual?

MEL: I have my moments.

WAN: *(Off file)* It says in the file that you were a sniper?

MEL: Yeah.

WAN: That's— …You must be a good shot.

MEL: I would hope.

WAN: When did you sign up?

MEL: Fall of '04.

(WAN looks up at MEL.)

WAN: 2004?

MEL: Yeah.

WAN: No military experience before that?

MEL: Nope.

WAN: And now you're out?

MEL: I had a four year contract.

WAN: *(Off the file again)* Okay. …And the incident with the teenager? *(He's just looking at her)* That you described in the questionnaire.

MEL: Did I use the word "teenager"?

WAN: You said he looked about sixteen or seventeen.

MEL: I think he was older.

WAN: I would imagine that was upsetting.

MEL: Kinda.

WAN: *(Off file)* It says here you declined psychiatric sessions upon your return.

MEL: Yeah.

WAN: Any particular reason?

(No answer)

WAN: Lance Corporal Anderson?

MEL: No.

WAN: Do you have problems sleeping *every* night?

MEL: Depends who I'm with.

WAN: Are you *in* a relationship?

MEL: No.

WAN: Would you characterize yourself as depressed? *(No answer)* Can I call you Mel?

MEL: I *want* you to call me Mel.

WAN: What made you sign up for the military, Mel?

MEL: What "made" me?

WAN: Yeah.

MEL: I got tired of having the TV tell me whatever fucked up thing our country had done that day on my behalf.

WAN: Okay.

MEL: I also thought it might be cool. *(Half-genuine)* I wanted to have a positive effect.

WAN: On—?

MEL: Things.

WAN: *(Nodding)* Okay. *(She writes in his file...then looks up.)* Are you willing to *talk* about the incident, Mel?

MEL: With *you?*

WAN: Yes.

MEL: Not really. *(Pause)* But it was pretty banal. If that's what you're fishing for. Not that different from the eight *other* guys I shot in the head.

(WAN regards MEL...)

WAN: Mel, this is just a very quick assessment—

MEL: Based on meeting me for five minutes—

WAN: Based on meeting you for five minutes, based on your file, based on my eight years experience in this field *and* based on how this war is affecting people in general, but my initial assessment is that it's not implausible that you're suffering from *some* sort of fallout from the incident with the, the *young* Iraqi man—about whom you don't want to talk. Not to mention the other eight.

(No answer)

WAN: Now before you get mad at me, let me tell you that there is a wide array of cutting edge treatments available right now with absolutely no stigma in receiving them—

MEL: What if I'm just a little sad?

WAN: *(A small smile)* The sadness gets treated too. It's one of our most popular symptoms.

MEL: Do you know how many guys in Iraq are getting Prozac shoved down their throat right now just so that they don't have to think about what they're doing?

WAN: I'm not sure that's true—

MEL: It's like forty percent—

WAN: I'm sensing a little resistance here—

MEL: *(Standing up)* It's actually rejection.

WAN: Bad memories *are* manageable—

MEL: I don't *wanna* manage my memory.

WAN: What do you want to do with it?—

MEL: Wear it around my fucking neck.

WAN: The therapies I'm talking about—

MEL: Let's be *real*—the only reason the army came up with "cutting edge therapies" is so that every time one of us shoots someone in the head, they give us a pill and we're back behind the sandbag next day. Right?—

WAN: That's not right—

MEL: I *don't want your drugs*—

WAN: Lance Corporal Anderson!—

MEL: *(Exiting)* Fuck you very much for the assessment, "Wanda"!—

(And he's gone...as lights shift—)

TAR: I appreciate your seeing me.

(Light finds the female actor, who has donned a military demeanor and now stands as SGT ANNE WILHELM, buttoned-down, very bright, kinda hot, in an efficient way. TAR stands before her...)

ANNE: It's my job. *(A small smile)* "Public Affairs."

TAR: *I'm* the public, *you're* the affair?

ANNE: Something like that, Mr... *(Off notepad)* —Al-Turki.

TAR: Call me T-Bone.

ANNE: That's okay.

(TAR's looking at her; she speaks while looking at notes.)

ANNE: So——in response to your request, I have the following information: During World War I, at the site known as the American University Experimental

Station in Washington D C, the U S Army *did* conduct
chemical warfare research. The area *behind* the
campus, now known as Spring Valley, *was* utilized as
a testing site. At the war's conclusion, *some* hazardous
substances were buried in the area. In 1993, these items
were discovered and unearthed, and sections of the
soil that tested positive for trace contamination were
remediated by the Army Corps of Engineers. The
Corps continues to stand by should other instances of
detection occur, which we're confident they won't.

(ANNE *looks up at* TAR, *who is watching and listening
carefully, not sure where to begin.*)

TAR: What were the traces of contamination?

ANNE: They were merely *traces*.

TAR: I know, but what were they?

ANNE: *(Off notes)* They were *traces* of chloride, cyanide,
ricin, Lewisite and mustard gas.

TAR: …Did people get sick from them?

ANNE: *(Off notes)* To the best of the Army's knowledge,
there have been no incidents of environmentally-
caused health problems as a result of the buried testing
equipment.

TAR: And what kind of stuff did they unearth?

ANNE: Ordnance.

TAR: Like—?

ANNE: Mortar rounds and 75-millimeter shells.

TAR: That were packed with chemical agents?

ANNE: Yes.

TAR: *(Beat)* What does it mean they "remediated the
soil"?

ANNE: Carted it away and replaced it with new soil. *If* the old was found to contain abnormally high levels of toxicity.

TAR: *(Pause)* And 1993's the only time they found stuff?

ANNE: *(Off notes)* Operation *Safe Removal* began in '93, extracting some 141 ordnance items using electromagnetic instruments. This took place over two years. In '95, the Corps declared Spring Valley safe.

(TAR's not sure what to ask next; ANNE plunges in, speaking to him quite directly.)

ANNE: Your interest in this is from having lived in Spring Valley as a child?

TAR: I still live there.

ANNE: And you've been in the U S all your life?

TAR: I don't look it?

ANNE: No—I was just—

TAR: I played Division One soccer.

ANNE: Is that true?

TAR: Yeah.

ANNE: Okay—well—I didn't mean to—

TAR: No, I know—

ANNE: Right. I just— Yes—you look it. You look American.

TAR: Thank you. You should see my underwear.

(A small truce; ANNE perhaps even smiles, intrigued by TAR's odd way of going about things, but still cautious.)

TAR: *(Extending his hand)* And for the record, I'm psyched about what you guys did to Saddam.

ANNE: ...Thank you.

TAR: You all got balls. My people are *from* that part of the world, so I can say that.

(ANNE *just looks at* TAR, *unsure whether he means all this, but it actually seems that he does. [And he does.] She nods*)

ANNE: Thank you.

(*Silence a moment*)

TAR: My dad has lived in Spring Valley for thirty-four years, in a house in which he is now *literally* withering away. Which I know because I sleep in the next room over and every morning there's less of him. And the fact is, we used to have a garden with tomatoes there. If it turns out he got cancer from living in a *chemical weapons dump*, it would be serious...*bullshit*. Would you agree?

ANNE: I very highly doubt that—

TAR: Did they do a health test? Like, of the local population?

ANNE: There isn't enough epidemiological evidence to justify the resources that would be required. In addition, the population is too low. One or two cases would skew the results and render the study meaningless. I'm sorry.

TAR: So then why are people filing a lawsuit?

ANNE: Because that's what people do. (*Pause*) But for your information, the army plans to schedule soil testing of all the houses in the area over the next several years, so I'm sure yours will come up. (*She stands, extends her hand.*) I sincerely hope your father gets better, Mr Al-Turki. Please consider my door open.

(TAR *looks at* ANNE, *and her hand...and turns to leave—*)

(*As lights find* BOB's—*and* MEL's—*apartment, as represented by a table;* BOB, *mid 50s, doesn't have a ponytail, but he probably once did. He is sitting at the table writing.* MEL *enters, looks for and finds a can of Coors Light.* BOB *looks at him, and then:)*

BOB: Hey there, kid.

MEL: Hey, Dad.

BOB: How did it go?

MEL: *("Upbeat")* Good.

BOB: Really? That's great.

MEL: Yeah.

BOB: So——? Did you—

MEL: Is it okay if we talk about it later?

BOB: …Sure.

(Beat; MEL *sips beer;* BOB *watches him, looking for a way in.)*

BOB: I was thinking of making those raviolis for dinner.

MEL: The, ah—?

BOB: Yeah. The porcini mushroom.

MEL: …Cool.

BOB: I talked to that editor today. The one who used to be with Harper Collins? He said he wants to look at this the second I finish.

MEL: Yeah?

BOB: Yeah. He's been shopping around the outline; thinks it's a surefire bet.

MEL: That's great.

BOB: It would be a dream. Complete dream come true.

MEL: I know. Quit the day job.

BOB: Well I don't know. Even if I *could*, it's not like the day job's not important.

MEL: It's true, Dad. The world needs you.

BOB: *(A smile)* That's right. Might not make it without me. Plus, of course, that's my subject matter. My *fodder.*

MEL: "The Environmentalist. A Love Story."

(BOB *again smiles.*)

BOB: You can joke, but this book could make a difference. *If* I do it right, it'll change things.

MEL: I'm just giving you shit.

BOB: *(Beat)* I keep thinking your mother's looking down on us, and then tapping at her watch and saying, "It's about fucking time, Bob."

MEL: Do you think she likes the fact that you make your son eat porcini mushroom ravioli like four times a week?

BOB: I think she'd be happy to know you're getting your selenium.

MEL: *(Beat)* I'm just curious, when you say she's "looking down on us," I'm assuming you mean from heaven?

BOB: Something like that.

MEL: Meaning you believe in, like, eternity?

BOB: I believe in spiritual *perseverance.*

MEL: Nice, Dad—

BOB: Thank you—

MEL: But not God?

BOB: I never said I don't believe in God.

MEL: Yeah you did.

BOB: When?

MEL: When I was six.

BOB: What'd I say?

MEL: You said, "Mel, I don't believe in God."

BOB: You sure I was talking about the *Big* God?

MEL: As opposed to—?

BOB: Oh you know... *(Small smile)* ...*Capitalism. (No answer...)* What is it, you want me to be Godless?

MEL: Sure.

(Beat)

BOB: Any luck on the job front?

MEL: Not a lot.

BOB: You'll find something.

MEL: Yeah, I just wanna, you know...

BOB: Take your time?

MEL: Yeah. Job market's not the same as...before.

BOB: You don't wanna call Bill? Go back to the carpentry—

MEL: I was a *carpenter's apprentice*, Dad.

BOB: Fine, but before that you were a financial analyst—

MEL: I know, and it was boring as shit.

BOB: *(Small smile)* Well *I* coulda told you that. *(Beat, as* BOB *looks at him...)* You're a good kid, Mel.

MEL: You too, Dad.

(Smile; beat; gentle:)

BOB: You think you'll go in for a *second* appointment?

MEL: Doubtful.

BOB: I don't think it's a bad idea.

MEL: I know you don't.

BOB: It's—

MEL: I said I know.

BOB: So *will* you?

MEL: I'm not sad, Dad.

BOB: That's not the point—

MEL: Yeah it is—

BOB: I've read up on the disease—

MEL: It's not a disease—

BOB: I read up on the *condition,* Mel, and you'll see that self-diagnosis is *very* difficult. *(No answer)* I'm saying this because I love you.

MEL: I got that part.

BOB: So then what's the problem? Because if it's a macho thing—

MEL: It's not a macho thing—

BOB: So if it's *not* a macho thing then I don't understand why you'd hesitate to take advantage of what they're—

MEL: The only reason you're telling me to do it is to prove your point that I was wrong-

BOB: That's not true—

MEL: Of course it is—

BOB: I'm saying it because I've watched you mope through life for the last four months and I just want you to do better. I want you to find a job you like and get a girlfriend and move out of my apartment—

MEL: See—

BOB: I'm kidding!—

MEL: No you're not—

BOB: You're right, I'm not!—

MEL: *See?!*—

BOB: But *you* don't even wanna live here—

MEL: Yeah I do—

BOB: Be serious, Mel—

MEL: I'm serious!—

BOB: Fine, I want you to live here, too, I just want you to be happy. I want you to be happy.

MEL: I'm happy.

BOB: You're happy?

MEL: Totally.

BOB: Good. *(Beat)* You know, you couldn't even get help for this kinda thing until about ten years after Vietnam.

MEL: *(Not overtly antagonistic)* How do *you* know?

BOB: Mel—

MEL: No, I'm just saying—

BOB: We're not gonna have this argument again, are—

MEL: Why not?

BOB: Because I thought we put it behind—

MEL: So then why're you bringing up the fucking Vietnam War? You can't invoke that because you have nothing to stand on because you didn't *go.*

BOB: Fine, Mel—

MEL: It's *not* fine, Dad, you're being a hypocrite—

BOB: *How?*—

MEL: By acting all "concerned" when in reality you disapprove of everything I stand for.

BOB: That's not—

MEL: You probably think I got what I deserved.

BOB: Absolutely not!—

MEL: You can admit it, Dad, because you've already accused me of signing up in order to piss you off.

BOB: *(Strong)* All I said was that there are inevitably numerous reasons why people, *all* people, do all kinds of things. Give me a little more credit than accusing you of acting like a one-year-old.

(No answer; gentle but insistent:)

BOB: Will you *think* about it? *(Pause)* A second appointment?

MEL: ...I'll see you later.

(MEL exits, leaving BOB standing there alone...as lights shift—)

(And we now find MEL at an empty bar, mid-afternoon. The female actor now returns as the bartender, who is actually CYNTH, the woman TAR was having sex with in the cemetery. She puts a bottle of Coors Light before him, takes his cash from the bartop and returns to her crossword puzzle as MEL sips and watches her. Beat...)

MEL: Excuse me, can I also get a shot of bourbon?

(CYNTH looks up; pause.)

CYNTH: What kind?

MEL: Ah...let's splurge and go with Jim Beam.

(CYNTH pours, not particularly impressed with his schtick; he waits, watching...)

MEL: You got a great smile.

(And it's pretty clear CYNTH hasn't smiled since he got there. She gives him the drink and takes a five from in front of him. Beat)

MEL: I don't want you to think I'm hitting on you... but...I *do* have a car. If you need a ride somewhere. After your...

CYNTH: Shift?

MEL: Yeah.

CYNTH: I'll keep that in mind.

(*Beat,* MEL *sips his Jim Beam...*)

MEL: You're new here.

CYNTH: You're intelligent.

MEL: (*A smile*) I'm looking for a job.

CYNTH: Is that right?

MEL: Yeah. Preferably something in international relations. Foreign service. World Bank. U N High Commission for Refugees. (*Pause*) But I'm also a very good short order. Chef.

CYNTH: *Cook?*

MEL: Yeah.

CYNTH: We don't serve food.

MEL: I know, but I could just be a...short order. Like you could give me short orders and I could...execute them.

(CYNTH*'s looking at* MEL.)

MEL: Or vice-versa. (*Pause*) If you're....

CYNTH: Into that?

MEL: Yeah.

CYNTH: No.

MEL: You don't have to answer now.

(CYNTH *"smiles," goes back to her puzzle...*)

MEL: Would you like me anymore if I told you I'd served our country? Two tours in Iraq?

CYNTH: No.

MEL: Not your favorite war?

CYNTH: No.

MEL: Me neither.

CYNTH: …So then why'd you go?

MEL: I wanted to liberate concentration camps.

(CYNTH's *just looking at* MEL.)

MEL: I *didn't*, by the way.

CYNTH: No, I hadn't heard that.

MEL: They had it on Fox, but…

CYNTH: Right.

MEL: How about…"I wanted to be part of the mechanism that was enacting decisions made on my behalf"?

CYNTH: …It's a *little* better.

(MEL *just sorta nods…*)

MEL: You do have a great smile.

CYNTH: When did you see me smile?

MEL: In my imagination.

(CYNTH *smiles a little.*)

MEL: Could I have another shot of Mr Beam?

(CYNTH *pours…*)

MEL: You ever *been* to Iraq?

CYNTH: Can't say I have.

MEL: *Any*where over there? Egypt? Jordan? Certain cross-dressing neighborhoods in *Yemen?* Lotta very good discos.

CYNTH: Sorry.

MEL: Very beautiful area that part of the world. Assuming you like palm groves and….body parts.

(CYNTH *doesn't smile.*)

MEL: Bad joke. *(Pause)* Don't worry, I've got a lot of them.

CYNTH: Maybe you should save 'em for therapy.

MEL: I thought this *was* therapy.

CYNTH: …You like your one-liners, don't you?

MEL: Not as much as my one-nighters.

CYNTH: Are you, like, *two?*

MEL: Yes. *(Pause)* Sorry. I have women issues. They all look the same to me. *(Pause)* Except you.

(CYNTH just looks at MEL….)

MEL: So do you *like* bartending?

CYNTH: No.

MEL: Then why do it? *(Pause)* I mean, you *sound* smart, in your lack of…actually talking to me; so it occurs to me you might be able to get a more—

CYNTH: High-profile job?

MEL: Yeah.

CYNTH: I like *this* bar.

MEL: Why?

CYNTH: 'Cause it's generally empty.

MEL: …What was it—bad relationship?

(No answer)

MEL: Well just remember……what goes around comes around. Or something like that.

(CYNTH just looks at MEL……as TAR walks in.)

TAR: What's up party people!?!

CYNTH: Hey—

TAR: Rock and roll!— *(Kissing her on the lips)* How are you?

CYNTH: Good.

TAR: You look totally hot.

CYNTH: No I don't—

TAR: Yeah you do. You make me wanna buy a car.

(CYNTH *just looks at* TAR)

TAR: *(To* MEL*)* What's up, man?

MEL: …What's up.

TAR: I'm T-Bone.

MEL: Mel.

TAR: What's up, Mel. *(Re:* CYNTH.*)* You meet Cynthia?
—She's my steady.

CYNTH: We've been out four times.

TAR: It's not about *time*, sugar-butt. *(To* MEL*)* This is the
loveliest bartender in northern Virginia. *(To* CYNTH*)*
Can I get a Coors Light?

CYNTH: No.

TAR: *(To* MEL*)* See? —She's got tremendous *chutzpa*.
Her old job was saving the world.

CYNTH: No, it wasn't.

TAR: Helping abused women. How 'bout a *Bud* Light?

CYNTH: Bottle or can?

TAR: *(To* MEL*)* She likes to ask me that 'cause she's
convinced the bottles are better but *I* know that the
bottles are bottled in, like Ohio or somewhere and they
don't have the same purity of water taste that the cans
do, which is ironic I know 'cause people in this country
look at cans, like, as a white trash thing, but— *(To*
CYNTH*)* I'll actually take a Pabst.

CYNTH: You think the water in *Saint Louis* is that much
purer than the water in Ohio?

TAR: The Mississippi River runs through St. Louis, Cynthia, which is *America's* river— *(To* MEL *with accent)* —"from what I understand of your literature."

*(*MEL *is just watching him stonefaced...*TAR *returns it, then turns back to* CYNTH.*)*

TAR: Anyhoodle.

CYNTH: *(Serving a Pabst)* So how did the Pentagon thing go?

TAR: It's a fucking *dead end.*

CYNTH: Why?—

TAR: Because the U S military is the biggest, blood thirstiest, most back-ass, savage, *pussy* organization in the entire, entire world. I mean the things this woman was telling me, I thought I was gonna puke. I'm watching my Dad die by inches and this chick's denying the possibility that it's even *linked*—like my Dad's public enemy number one, and I just wanted to be like, *"Eat me,* my dad never hurt a *fly!"* And I'm sorry 'cause I know you like this country and you've got relatives here and you're really into, you know, *Tivo,* but this place is a ridiculous, hypocritical, total fucking wasteland. *(Turning to* MEL*)* I hope none of this offends you.

MEL: I wasn't really listening.

*(*TAR *stares at* MEL*...then turns back to* CYNTH.*)*

TAR: Anyway.

CYNTH: I'm sorry.

TAR: *They're* the ones who should apologize. But they can't; they can't even say "sorry". I mean...it makes the whole country come off as a big, gaping anus hole.

(Out of nowhere, MEL *sneezes without, it seems, covering his mouth.* TAR *looks back at him; pause)*

TAR: Can you cover your mouth?

MEL: I did.

TAR: No you didn't.

MEL: Yeah I did.

TAR: *(Pause)* No, you didn't.

MEL: Dude.

TAR: What?

MEL: I covered my mouth.

(MEL *and* TAR *stare at one another…*)

TAR: Do you got a problem?

MEL: No. Do you?

TAR: No.

MEL: So then stop fucking looking at me.

TAR: Woah, woah—I think you need to stop talking like that and I think you need to apologize for sneezing on her.

MEL: I didn't sneeze on her—

TAR: Did you cover your mouth?

MEL: I have no idea what you're all pissed off about, but you should seriously stop talking to me before you regret walking in here like an asshole.

CYNTH: Guys—

TAR: *What'd* you say?

MEL: I said I will destroy your face and I'm not fucking around.

CYNTH: Tariq, back off.

TAR: *What?*

CYNTH: Go to the corner, seriously, go away—

TAR: Why should I go to the corner when this dickwad can't apologize for not covering his mouth—

MEL: *(Standing up)* Don't call me a dickwad—

TAR: You're a *total* dickwad—

MEL: Don't call me dickwad—

TAR: *DICK—WAD—*

CYNTH: You guys are being idiots—

TAR: Cynthia.

CYNTH: T-Bone—

TAR: Cynthia—

MEL: *"T-Bone"?*

CYNTH: What?

TAR: I can handle this. *(To* MEL, *with deliberation:)* Listen to me, dickwad—

*(*MEL *violently shoves* TAR *in the chest with both hands, which causes* TAR *to lose his balance and send his stool toppling backwards.* CYNTH *scoots around the bar to get in between the two, as* TAR *pops up ready to go after* MEL, *who stands ready and waiting. A mini-standoff—as* CYNTH *speaks to* MEL*)*

CYNTH: Can you please leave the bar?

*(*CYNTH *hands* MEL *his money from the bar top.)*

CYNTH: Now. Take your money, leave the bar. Or I'll call the police on *both* of you.

*(*MEL *waits.)*

CYNTH: I'm serious. Get the fuck out. *Now.*

*(…*MEL *declines to take the money…and turns and leaves… Silence;* CYNTH *turns to* TAR.*)*

CYNTH: *(Incredulous)* Why'd you do that?

TAR: Do what?

CYNTH: That was *idiotic.*

TAR: He was being a jerk.

CYNTH: So were you. *(She straightens up...)*

TAR: You're mad?

CYNTH: I *shouldn't* be? *(Silence)* So what are you gonna do? About the Pentagon?

TAR: Nothing. It's the U S military. You think they're gonna change how they do things cause some fucked up Arab dude strolls into their office?

CYNTH: I just think what they did is messed up.

TAR: Don't be pissed at *me.*

CYNTH: I'm not, but I mean, *you're* obviously pissed off, and yet the only person you're gonna act out against is some guy who accidentally sneezes near you at a bar?

TAR: I have subtle ways of channeling my rage. Same case could be made for you. *(Pause)* I mean, your brother dies and the most you do is quit your job.

CYNTH: Who was I supposed be pissed at—the *germs*?

TAR: I'm just saying. You're not exactly the poster-girl for how to live life.

CYNTH: Yeah, well......maybe *neither* of us is burdened by ambition.

*(—*TAR *takes this in......as lights shift—)*

TAR: Thanks for seeing me again.

(And we find TARiq *standing before* ANNE, *the Pentagon public affairs person.)*

ANNE: Anything for a Division One soccer player. So what can I do for you?

TAR: *(Strong)* I want you guys to soil-sample my house. I want the army to test my house to see if there are chemicals in the ground.

ANNE: The army is scheduled to test all the houses—

TAR: I want mine done now. I want you to expedite it.

(ANNE *stares at* TAR *for a moment...*)

ANNE: Remind me of the address?

TAR: 478 Glenbrooke Road.

(ANNE *pulls a file, looks through it...*)

ANNE: It's scheduled for next year.

TAR: I want it done now. This week.

(ANNE *looks at* TAR, *not that impressed; he presses on.*)

TAR: My father was with the Saudi Arabian Embassy—
here in D.C. He was *not* an insignificant man. Do you
know what'll happen if I start telling people he's dying
because of chemical weapons buried in his own back
yard? (*Starting to lose it*) I have *one* memory of my
father with a smile on his face; he's eating a tomato.
And I wanna know if that tomato killed him. I wanna
know if the U S military poisoned my dad's blood with
a tomato, because if they did, it's fucking *bullshit* and I
deserve to know the truth.

ANNE: (*Beat*) Your father was a chauffeur.

(*Silence as* TAR *just stares at* ANNE)

TAR: I realize that.

ANNE: Which is not to say he was insignificant. Or that
your...*allegation* is meaningless. But it *does* mean you
shouldn't come in here threatening me.

TAR: (*Beat; stoic:*) How did you know who my father
was?

ANNE: This isn't a Ma and Pa joint, Mr Al-Turki. A
peculiar-acting Saudi national comes to my office
asking about buried chemical weapons, you don't
think I'm gonna prick up my little ears? (*She opens a
drawer and produces a file.*) I had them run you through

the computers at Langley. We debated arresting you for obscene gesturing, public fornication, habitual public urination…but we ultimately felt we should spend our efforts on people more threatening to our national security. *(Looking up)* So I'm pleased to report we don't think you're a terrorist.

TAR: You guys are freaks.

ANNE: Yes we are.

(Beat…TAR leans in, intense:)

TAR: I wanna know if you're gonna test my house.

ANNE: I'm curious if you speak Arabic, Mr. Al-Turki.

TAR: Only when I'm urinating in public. Are you gonna test my house?

ANNE: *Do* you speak Arabic?

TAR: You can't ask me that! *(Pause)* A bit.

ANNE: I'll see what I can do.

(ANNE leaves TAR alone…)

(—as light comes up on BOB, drinking coffee at the table in his apartment. MEL enters…)

MEL: Hey, Dad.

BOB: Hey.

(MEL takes a six pack of Tecate beer cans, out of a plastic bag.)

MEL: I, ah…I got the kind of beer you like.

(BOB looks at the beer, then at MEL…)

BOB: *(Honest)* Thank you.

MEL: You're welcome.

BOB: *(Beat)* What've you been up to?

MEL: Not much. *(Pause)* They got a new bartender at George's.

BOB: What happened to Ron?

MEL: Gone.

BOB: Is the new guy nice?

MEL: Girl. Woman. Empowered homo sapien. *(Pause)* I know you don't like me goin' to bars.

BOB: I don't mind you going to the occasional bar, Mel, I just think that every afternoon is a little excessive.

MEL: ...It was *late* afternoon.

BOB: You should come with me to the gym tomorrow.

MEL: I'm not really a big gym guy.

BOB: It's good for you. And as much as it may *feel* like it, five hours a day of *Donkey Kong* won't keep you in shape.

MEL: It's not *Donkey Kong,* Dad.

BOB: Well, what*ever* that game is.

MEL: *(Beat)* How was work?

BOB: *(Not usually asked)* It was good.

MEL: Was the world incredibly toxic today?

BOB: *(A smile)* Yes—the world was pretty toxic. It's all I can do to clean up my little corner of it.

(Beat; MEL sips beer.)

MEL: I wanted to say. In terms of what we were talking about the other day? I just wanted to say that there's a part of me that thinks what you did was good. Or brave or whatever. In terms of Vietnam.

BOB: Okay...

MEL: By going to jail for it.

BOB: ...Thank you. *(Beat)* And the *other* part of you?

MEL: Wishes you had fought.

BOB: Why?

MEL: So that you'd know what I'm going through.

BOB: I know. But…that's the choice you made, Mel. In the face of a lot of people telling you not to.

MEL: People didn't tell *you* not to go to jail back then?

BOB: Of course they did—

MEL: But you acted on conviction.

BOB: Yes—

MEL: And then you turned around and taught *me* to always do that.

BOB: Absolutely—

MEL: So then stop giving me shit for what I've done—

BOB: Mel, it is fine to have conviction about wanting to improve what you see going on out there—and I will *happily* take credit for teaching you that—but you lose the argument when you step into a war so *clearly* being run with an utter lack of competence.

MEL: Whereas *your* choice would be to just sit back and let it *fully* fall to shit.

BOB: Oh c'mon—

MEL: We were *there,* Dad; it was our responsibility to fix our mistakes.

BOB: It wasn't *your* responsibility—

MEL: Why *not* me? Someone at least *trying* to affect how things get done.

BOB: And did you, Mel—*did* you affect the war from your "insert position"?

MEL: I tried—

BOB: By being a *sniper?*

MEL: Yes—by designing my own missions, by learning how a neighborhood works, by *talking* with the people and asking them to trust me so that I could *help* them—

BOB: Well that's where you lose me. Because I don't think it's possible to positively affect a system that's *designed* for destruction.

MEL: Oh c'mon, Dad, it's *your* argument: To change how a mechanism works, it helps to be *inside* it.

BOB: I agree—

MEL: I mean look around, all you've been talking about with this election is "the people wanted change" —well it's the same thing I was trying to do: Change from within!

BOB: Fine, but then don't come back here blaming everyone else for how you feel.

MEL: Who am I blaming?!

BOB: You're blaming me, Mel, you're sitting here indicting me for how I've lived my life—

MEL: That's not true—

BOB: Well that's how I *feel*. *(Beat; silence)* But more importantly......as a result of your efforts, there has been damage. To yourself. Which you have to take care of—

(MEL hurls his beer at the wall.)

BOB: And I'm not gonna *stop* saying that just because it makes you uncomfortable.

MEL: Fine.

BOB: *And*—if you're not gonna help your*self*, then maybe *I'm* not the best...I'm not the best person to be of assistance. *(Pause)* Even though I want to.

(MEL looks at BOB...)

BOB: The question, Mel, is no longer, "Do you believe in what you did?" It's: "What the hell are you gonna do *now?*

(Tense silence for a moment…and then BOB *hands* MEL *a piece of paper:)*

BOB: I got this off the V A website. He's a former paratrooper or something. He's talking on Thursday. About brain stuff. I thought it might be interesting.

*(*MEL *looks at the paper.)*

*(*BOB *hands* MEL *the paper, stands and leaves……)*

(…as lights crossfade to TAR, *standing in his Spring Valley backyard…. Lights shift again to reveal that* CYNTH *is next to him, and they are both there watching* BOB, *who is on a knee, taking soil samples, or perhaps having just finished)*

BOB: What I've done is take samples from four areas around the yard, each at varying depths.

TAR: How deep for each one?

BOB: We bore down to six feet and test it every foot.

CYNTH: For arsenic?

BOB: Exactly.

TAR: When does the cleanup goal kick in?

BOB: At 43 parts per million, but for *this* neighborhood, due to the controversy, it's 12-per-million.

TAR: And if that comes back positive—?

BOB: We'd do a more in-depth grid. That's why your house wasn't scheduled 'til next year. It's a slow process. *(He writes on his clipboard, and then:)* How long you lived here?

TAR: My dad since '74. Off and on for me.

BOB: Where're you from? Originally?

TAR: Saudi Arabia. My dad was with the embassy.

BOB: Your dad was with the Saudi Embassy?

TAR: Yeah.

CYNTH: The lady from the Pentagon said that the Army Corps of Engineers were the ones who were dealing with this stuff.

BOB: They're the ones overseeing it. They contract out *my* company to do the actual testing. Basically we're a bunch of tree-huggers who the army uses for P R purposes. *They* get to look good and *we* get to force them to clean up their mess. Environmentally speaking. *(Beat; casual)* So what's it been like being an Arab in the middle of all this?

TAR: Of all what?

BOB: The war.

TAR: Hasn't really affected me that much.

BOB: People don't give you a hard time?

TAR: Not really. A little, I guess.

CYNTH: He's one of those Arabs who listens to *Supertramp*.

BOB: *(A confused smile)* How about being the son of a Saudi diplomat? Does that get...complicated?

TAR: My father was the embassy chauffeur.

BOB: Hey, that's complicated, too. Listen, my son Mel signed up for the marines and *fought* in Iraq. Majored in economics and became a *sniper. Killed* people. And look at me, I think the war's goddam despicable.

TAR: I guess I'm just not really political.

BOB: Everyone's political, it's just a matter of realizing it. What do you do? For a living?

TAR: I, ah......I drive also.

BOB: Oh, is that the car out there?

TAR: Yeah; it was my Dad's, actually. The embassy let us keep it when he retired.

BOB: It's *certainly* a relic. People must love that.

TAR: Yeah.

BOB: And I imagine it makes your Dad proud. That you use it.

TAR: …I think it's more that he just likes having me around.

BOB: Right. *(Off his clipboard)* Okay then, I think I'm done here. *(He's looking around.)* It's a pretty nice house for a chauffeur.

CYNTH: He was a *Saudi* chauffeur.

BOB: *(With a smile)* That's right. He still in America?

TAR: Yeah.

CYNTH: Tariq actually just checked him into a hospital yesterday. He's got blood cancer.

BOB: *(Realizing)* Oh—I'm sorry.

TAR: Hey.

BOB: There's a lawsuit, you know. I'd probably get in trouble for telling you—

TAR: We heard about it.

BOB: *(To* CYNTH*)* You gonna be a part of it?

CYNTH: Actually—-we're not married.

BOB: Oh, I see. *(To* TAR*)* Are *you*?

TAR: I was gonna see what happens with the soil.

BOB: You don't need *that* to be political. You should join it. From what I understand there are meetings every month. Here— *(Handing him his card)* —call me if you ever decide to go. I'll tell you all the *other* screwed up environmental stuff the army's done in this country.

*(*TAR *nods…)*

BOB: Anyway…nice talkin' to you-—

TAR: You too.

CYNTH: You said your son was a Marine?

BOB: I did.

CYNTH: What's his name again?

BOB: Mel. Why?

CYNTH: …Wow—

BOB: What?

CYNTH: I think I've seen him in my bar.

BOB: You work at George's? In Fairfax?

CYNTH: Yeah—

BOB: You're the new Ron?

CYNTH: I'm the new Ron.

BOB: Well. I'll be. It's a small goddamned world.

(*—as lights pop up on* CHUCK CAROUSO *[played by the actor who plays* BOB, *who is his antithesis], mid-speech with a handheld microphone, dressed in civvies, his delivery is all military brusqueness with a touch of with new age tenderness. [Perhaps we only hear the first couple lines, followed by our seeing* CHUCK *with the mike].*)

CHUCK: Soldiers, it's now *scientifically documented* that if your right motor cortex gets annihilated in a car accident, your *left* motor cortex can be trained to step up and save the day. It is *documented* that if you jab a needle in your brain you will generate *significant* electrical activity. It is *documented* that when you place a monk in an MRI and have him do what monks do, you *will* witness this monk literally *re*-wire his own hardwiring and *transform* his mind. (*Beat for effect*) Neuroplasticity is *in* our court, folks, all we have to do is *bounce the frickin' ball.* And I'm not talkin' new-age lingo here, people; this isn't "The Secret," Okay? — Although *yes* there's the "power of positive thought,"

and *sure* there's "neurobics" and of *course* there are
sixty "brain-awakening" exercises that you can read
about in the New York frickin' times, none of which
I'm denigrating. Except for *The New York Times.* But
seriously—thank you—but what *I'm* talking about is
human beings *proactively* rewiring their brains. And
do you wanna know the only thing that's stopping us
from doing that?

(From off-stage the female actor shouts—)

FEMALE: *(O S)* OUR *SELVES!!!*

CHUCK: That's right. *Our. Selves. (With a wink)* She
comes to *all* my stuff. *(calmer:)* Neuroplasticity *example*:
Young man in a vicious knife fight, Weymouth,
Massachusetts. Paralyzed from the shoulders down.
But instead of giving up, he puts his brain to work. Do
you want to know what this young man does now?

Female: *TELL US, CHUCK!*

CHUCK: He opens e-mails with his *thoughts.* You
think that's cute?—hear me out: The doctor sticks
a sensor with a hundred tiny electrodes into this
guy's motor cortex; that sensor is then connected to a
neural interface decoder, which in turn is connected
to a computer cursor—which he *controls* and opens
the e-mail with. *Intention*, separate from the physical
body, achieving its goal. *(Honest)* That is revolutionary.
(As he profoundly switches gears—) My name is Chuck
Carouso. In 1995 I jumped out of an airplane as part
of a military training exercise over the Smoke Creek
Desert in Nevada. Eight seconds into the jump I
collided with another member of my unit, each of
us going approximately a hundred and twenty-five
miles an hour. His left boot impacted the back of my
neck, just below my helmet, causing my spinal cord to
crush up against my cerebral cortex. I immediately lost
consciousness and the only reason I'm standing here

today is because that same noble team member was able to pull my cord and cradle me as we floated to the desert floor. *(Beat)* I was unconscious for a week and my wife was told I'd have irrevocable brain damage. *(He looks over his audience)* When I woke up, I didn't recognize my wife; I couldn't say the alphabet and when I looked at the T V, I thought Bill Clinton seemed like a nice guy. *(He winks, then holds for possible applause. He now becomes serious—and convincing:)* I was un-homed. As a result of physical injury, I was mentally… *and* emotionally—lost. *(Pause)* Do any of you soldiers out there know what it's like to be emotionally un-homed? They got a phrase for this in German: *Un Heimlich.* Un-homed. A million miles away. *(Quiet, almost soft:)* But there *are* ways back. Neural pathways, ignited by intention. E M D R therapy, *virtual reality* therapy, a new clinical trial that treats P T S D with *ecstasy.* Point is, for those of you out there with *different* injuries. Whose damage isn't *physical.* My message is: It is your *physiology*—that will bring you home. *(Hushed)* Thank you.

(Lights find MEL, *standing to the side, having just heard this speech. He approaches* CHUCK—*)*

MEL: Hi.

CHUCK: How're you doin'?

MEL: I really enjoyed your speech.

CHUCK: Thank you.

MEL: Especially the part about people being unhomed.

CHUCK: My pleasure. You just back from in-theater?

MEL: Yes sir. About four months.

CHUCK: *(Extending his hand)* From one vet to another: Thanks for serving, son.

(Pause, as MEL *takes this in…)*

MEL: Can I ask you something?

CHUCK: *(Glances at watch)* If you make it snappy.

MEL: I'm wondering if you think I should've missed.

CHUCK: Not sure I'm following, son.

MEL: I always read that soldiers did that. Miss on purpose, at the last second. *(Pause)* But I didn't.

CHUCK: ...And why do you think that is?

MEL: ...'Cause my team member woulda' given me shit. *(Pause)* 'Cause the guy I shot was laying a bomb that woulda' killed people I'd been eating hamburgers with for seven months. *(Pause)* But the thing is, none of my *other* kills are buggin' me.

CHUCK: You were doing your job, soldier. Saving people's lives.

MEL: I know. But then why do I feel like such a...a dickwad?

CHUCK: You're not a dickwad.

MEL: *(Quiet)* I didn't kill fifty people. *(Still quieter)* But my head's not right. ......I can't keep my head straight.

(CHUCK looks at him; it's pretty obvious he's hurting. He checks his watch, then speaks to MEL in a strong but gentle voice)

CHUCK: You wanna know what America's good at? Solving problems. We excel at that. Even if *we're* occasionally the cause. And what we have here is a problem. But what we also have are solutions. Unlike other countries, we don't just sit around complaining. We fucking *fix* things. *(Pause)* You need to find a path, son—

MEL: Yes—

CHUCK: That will *guide* you home.

(zeroing in with supreme, hushed intensity, perhaps even taking Mel's head in his hands:)

CHUCK: And everytime you think this is self-involved, naval-gazing *crap*, remember this: *(Re: his head)* The world in *here*, is intimately connected to the world out *there*. Meaning we're all in this together. So to change *your* world…is to change *the* world. *(Pause)* And isn't that what you signed up for in the first place?

MEL: Yes.

(—as music fades up, MEL stands very still, and we see that he has truly listened for perhaps the first time in this play.)

CHUCK: Don't worry, son. We'll get you through this.

(Lights shift…as the music swells………and continues…… and eventually lands us—)

(With Mel, who now stands in narrow light; to aud:)

MEL: When my unit got back from Iraq, the commanders were so worried about our "psychological decompression" that they instead completely embarrassed us. Or at least me. They flew us back to Camp Lejeune for forty-eight hours without letting us see our families; then they flew *my* group to Northern Virginia where they assembled all our families in this huge basketball arena and "pre"-hyped them up to cheer like maniacs, at which point they turned out the lights, announced us like a football team and had us run through the tunnel that leads to the court as they blared *Eye Of The Tiger*; total rah-rah Henry Five bullshit, completely ridiculous considering all we wanted to do was hug our mothers in private. Or in my case, my Dad. *(Beat)* It was actually the moment I hugged my dad that I knew there was something…*off*.

(As lights shift…)

(—and find MEL on a chair, opposite SALLY, a civilian therapist— [played by female actor] —who sits on a chair

directly facing him— [or perhaps, more abstractly, they are
both facing out to the audience.] She is attentive, caring, and
at first a touch crunchy)

SAL: Hi, Mel, I'm Sally.

MEL: Hi, Sally.

SAL: Hi, Mel. You were referred by Chuck Carouso?

MEL: Yeah.

SAL: I love that man. He's dreamy.

MEL: He called you a "really viable path."

SAL: I am. It's great you're here.

MEL: Good.

SAL: It's *great*, actually. So tell me how much you know
about E M D R.

MEL: I know *nothing* about E M D R.

SAL: That's *OKAY*. It stands for Eye Movement
Desensitization and Reprocessing, which has been
used with *remarkable* results in Oklahoma City, the
Balkans, Columbine, post-earthquake Bangladesh and
of course after 9/11. Really all over; it truly *is* the wave
of the future for mental trauma treatment.

MEL: …Good.

SAL: Don't be cynical, Mel—

MEL: I'm not—

SAL: It's OK if you are, cynicism is part of the game
that we're here to deconstruct.

MEL: …Cool.

SAL: E M D R works with memory networks, Mel, by
forging a relationship between the distressing memory,
on one hand—and more *adaptive* information contained
in *other* memory networks on the *other* hand. When
that relationship occurs, new connections are made,

this time from positive information, rather than just negative. E M D R literally dislodges the traumatic memory from the nervous system, deals with it, and helps you move on.

MEL: Gotcha.

SAL: You can smirk about it but it works. *(Convincing:)* This shit works, Mel.

(MEL has no answer to this.)

SAL: What we'll do first is target identification.

MEL: Umm…a big store with headquarters in Canada.

SAL: *(Laughing)* That's very funny, I've never heard that one…. *(But now all business)* —Okay, I want you to find in your head the event that most disturbs you from Iraq. *(She waits.)* Do you have an image?

MEL: Yeah.

SAL: Okay. Now I want you to tell me the most negative thing you can think of *regarding* that image.

MEL: *(Pause)* His body. Beneath the overpass. *(Pause)* Silence.

SAL: Good. Keep concentrating on it, and try to remember as much detail about it as you can. The most vivid, visual image of it as you can. Don't *tell* me, just find those details and hold them in your head. *(She waits.)* How're we doing?

MEL: We're doing swell.

SAL: Good. *(Pause…)* Now I want you to tell me a belief you've formed about yourself in regard to that image.

MEL: …I'm a dickwad.

SAL: Okay. Good. Now choose a positive belief that you'd like to replace the negative one with.

MEL: I'm a dickwad but I've kept my sense of humor.

SAL: Be more positive.

MEL: I love myself to the point where it's unhealthy.

SAL: Mel. Think harder.

MEL: *(Pause)* I would like to…do better things. *(Pause)* With my life.

SAL: *(Genuine)* Good. *(Beat)* Now this is all we're going to do for today. We're just going to talk about those two beliefs. It's not until our next session that we'll begin the actual reprocessing.

MEL: Which entails what?

SAL: Which entails moving my finger in front of your eyes so that we simulate what you do in REM sleep. And we're gonna *use* that method to *process* the event; the same way a dream processes an average day. We're gonna dislodge the memory, Mel, with all its disturbing imagery, and we're gonna attach to it some *positive* associations. *(Pause)* So that you can live with it. *(Pause)* At which point you'll be on your way.

(…off MEL—*)*

(—as lights shift to the bar, where BOB, TAR *and* CYNTH *are mid-conversation, drinking cans of Coors Light.* BOB *is deep into Noam Chomsky/ex-hippie mode.)*

BOB: And thus I needn't enlighten you as to the *extraordinary* intimacy between the Saudi government and *ours*, beginning with Franklin "Polio-Boy" Roosevelt's 1945 tet-a-tete with *your* founder and first king, Ibn frickin' Saud!

TAR: You're talking way too much, Bob—

BOB: *I know!*—the point is: we are in a war about oil gussied up as a war about chemical weapons that were never found except for *here* in the backyard of *your* Saudi father's house! It's no *wonder* you're a deer-in-the-headlights!

CYNTH: Yeah, but his Dad *isn't* part of the monarchy. So he's not really—

BOB: Actually, Cynthia—he *is*. *He's* the monarchy because we're *ALL* the monarchy—meta-hypa-phorically. We're *all* a part of it.

CYNTH: Of what?

BOB: Of a world that's boinking itself in the ass, pardon my Turkish. A world in which the U S-Saudi link is merely the most *obvious* manifestation of the fact that we're *all* in some way culpable.

TAR: Bob, you should switch to light beer.

BOB: You think I'm joking?

CYNTH: I'm just not sure what you can do about it.

BOB: You start by doing what you did today.

TAR: What—sit on folding chairs and listen to people rant?

BOB: Legal recourse can change the world, T-Bone. It's a form of fighting back.

CYNTH: No, Bob, lawsuits are a potentially lucrative form of anger management.

BOB: Fine, but they're also an action linked to something greater than yourself.

CYNTH: How?

BOB: Because you're fighting from within the belly of the beast. And if you do it correctly——it is an infectious, self-generating *power*. *You* saw those people today—fire in their eyes, and it was in *your* eyes, too, I could see it.

TAR: I dunno, Bob—

BOB: You have an *obligation*, T-Bone.

TAR: Why?

BOB: Because no doubt, your father is a gentle man, but he too is inextricably linked to the mechanism I'm talking about. He spent his life driving the *Saudi ambassador* up and down the streets of D C. To fancy lunches, to oil lobby meetings, to the White House. And with the money he earned, he bought a nice house and he got a nice car, which *you* now drive. And I'm not just blaming you; it's *all* of us; all of us in this room are participants in and beneficiaries of that power structure.

CYNTH: The power structure that—?

BOB: The power structure that employs *violence for the sake of luxury!* And it is our job to fight against it—even it's just by going to lonely little lawsuit meetings. It's not just a *personal* act, Tariq. It's political.

CYNTH: *(Beat…)* Tariq?

(TAR isn't answering. BOB and CYNTH look at him but he is looking down, away from them, lost in thought……)

CYNTH: You all right?

(TAR nods but doesn't answer. All is quiet for a moment………after which TAR gathers himself, embarrassed…….)

TAR: *(Quiet)* Yeah. I was just……you said something about my Dad, which sort of……I don't know.

CYNTH: What was it?

TAR: About him driving up and down the streets of D C.

CYNTH: *(Pause)* Why was that…?

TAR: I dunno; it's just……sometimes I feel like that's all I do. *(Beat)* The doctor told me they wanna move him to a hospice. My Dad.

CYNTH: When did he say that?

TAR: This morning. *(Pause)* They think it's time...for that to happen.

BOB: I'm so sorry to hear that.

TAR: I knew it was coming. *(Beat)* Anyway.

(CYNTH puts her hands on TAR's; beats......)

BOB: *(Off his watch)* I suppose this is about the time my son usually stops by, no?

CYNTH: That would be true.

TAR: Really?

CYNTH: Yeah.

TAR: Maybe I shouldn't be here, Bob.

BOB: Why not?

TAR: Well you know. Me and your son. Lotta tension. The whole fight thing.

BOB: The fight about the sneeze?

TAR: Yeah.

BOB: Oh c'mon, T-Bone. Give my boy a little slack., he's going through a real rough patch—

TAR: I'm not saying he's not—

BOB: Good, so cut him a little slack.

TAR: *(Beat; to CYNTH)* He comes in here everyday?

CYNTH: They live down the street. He's a nice guy.

TAR: Fine. *(Pause, then half a smile:)* But only 'cause we're all a part of it, Bob.

BOB: Exactly. *(Having fun)* Right, Cynthia?

CYNTH: Only on weekends.

BOB: Oh c'mon—you can't be *that* cynical.

CYNTH: It's not cynicism; it's just wanting to curb your optimism.

BOB: Why?

CYNTH: Because there's been a lot of damage.

BOB: I agree. Look at my son.

CYNTH: Exactly. So it's hard not to be cynical when you realize that no one really cares anymore. That amidst all the excitement of a "brand new world", he could just be forgotten. *(Pause)* Which is too bad; because what he did was pretty fucking noble.

(Beat; TAR takes this in)

BOB: *(Honest)* I agree. *(Raising his glass)* Cheers.

(The others toast; BOB drains his can.)

BOB: I don't think I've had this much beer since 1978.

TAR: You need to switch to tequila, Robert.

(MEL enters; he sees the three of them there....)

MEL: Hey.

BOB: Hey, Mel! C'mon in.

(MEL takes a step or two in; hesitant)

MEL: What's up?

BOB: Mel, you know Cynthia, of course, and I guess you also know T-Bone here—

MEL: Yeah.

BOB: He's the one I was telling you about, with the maybe-toxic soil.

MEL: That's *him*?

BOB: That's him.

(Beat)

MEL: *(Neutral)* What're you doing here Dad?

BOB: Just shooting the shit. T-Bone's from Saudi Arabia, which I just love.

MEL: You "love" that?

BOB: Yeah, you know, people's countries of origen…. always fascinating.

(MEL *just nods; beat; then, softer, to* CYNTH)

MEL: How're you doin'?

CYNTH: Good.

(TAR *is watching their interaction closely*)

MEL: Bar's not so empty today.

CYNTH: No.

MEL: I like it better that way, too.

(CYNTH *has poured him a shot, which he now drinks; awkward silence as* MEL *looks at her, a small, non-aggressive smile, like he knows her inside out.*)

MEL: Anyway, I should get going.

BOB: You just got here.

MEL: I know, but…time's a-wastin'.

BOB: No it's not, Mel.

MEL: I was just gonna do a shot and go home. Look for a job.

BOB: Should I come with?

MEL: Stay. *(Neutral)* Seriously.

BOB: Mel—

MEL: I'm serious.

(*He starts for the door, then turns back*)

MEL: *(To* TAR:) You having a good time?

TAR: Good enough.

MEL: Good. *(Heading for door)* Have fun.

(*As* MEL *exits. Silence…*)

BOB: I should probably go with him.

(BOB *gets his coat;* CYNTH *gives him a small, genuine smile.*)

CYNTH: Thanks for taking us to the meeting.

BOB: Sure thing. *(Before leaving) Join that lawsuit, T-Bone.*

TAR: Right.

CYNTH: 'Bye, Bob.

BOB: Bye now.

(BOB *exits.* TAR *watches* CYNTH, *who watches the door...*)

TAR: You all right?

CYNTH: Yeah. You?

TAR: Yeah.

CYNTH: *(Beat)* The guy's just a customer. His son.

TAR: Who said he wasn't?

(They sit in silence a moment...)

(—as lights shift back to SAL *the E M D R instructor's office, where* MEL *again sits before her as she somewhat rapidly moves her finger back and forth in front of his eyes, which follow the movement)*

SAL: Keep following, Mel.... Just notice what comes to mind...

(SAL continues for perhaps 10 seconds before stopping; MEL *blinks out the sensation... Beat)*

SAL: What are you getting?

MEL: The same event.

SAL: The body beneath the overpass?

MEL: Yeah.

SAL: Okay. Now let your mind go blank......and describe to me your feelings in regard to that.

MEL: Besides the dickwad feeling?

SAL: I want you to tell me *why* you think that keeps coming up.

MEL: Because I killed someone. *(Pause)* A teenager.

SAL: Okay. *(Beat)* So our goal, now, Mel, is going to be to try to displace the dickwad feeling—in large part, by attaching a *positive* belief to that image. To the image of that kid.

MEL: There is no positive belief, Sallie. I blew the entire back of his head off.

SAL: …I understand.

MEL: No you don't—because *you're* not seeing the details.

SAL: Do you want to describe them to me?—

MEL: No.

SAL: Okay. You don't have to. They're *your* details, Mel. It doesn't matter how much of them *I* know. My job is simply to help you create more positive associations with their memory.

MEL: There are none.

SAL: What about the idea we talked about last time? The idea of doing better things with your life.

MEL: I don't really think that's doable.

SAL: *(Pause)* You don't think it's *possible* that there are things you're going do in your life from here on out, *good* things, that you would never have done had you not gone to Iraq? *(Pause)* That you actually might, as a *result* of having killed that kid that day, end up doing *better* things? With your life. Specifically *because* of what you did to him?

MEL: *(Eyes closed)* …I don't know.

SAL: Well that's what I want you to focus on this time. As we go through this again. I just want you to contemplate that notion. That your life, and maybe even *other* people's lives, can gain, as a result of that loss. That there exists the *possibility* that you, Mel, will end up doing very good things; *because* of what you did.

(MEL *just sits there, eyes still closed*)

(*After a moment he opens them, trying to try*)

SAL: This is how people get better, Mel. (*She raises her finger...*) So just focus on that image. Of you doing good. It's not too late.

(MEL *looks at* SAL*...and she begins the rapid finger movement again...for perhaps 10 seconds...until he suddenly stands unable to continue*)

MEL: ......I have to put some money in the meter.

(*...as lights now find* TAR *standing in the office of* ANNE, *the Pentagon Public Affairs officer played by female actor.*)

ANNE: I received the results of the soil sampling from the 478 Glenbrooke residence. It seems that several of the samples *did* test above the 12-part median, meaning further grid work was conducted, at which point it was determined that none of those surpassed the 43 parts per million point at which cancer rates would increase by one in ten-thousand.

TAR: ...Meaning *what*?

ANNE: Meaning at this time we *will* remediate the land, but there is simply *not* enough toxic soil to conclusively conclude that your family was exposed to dangerous levels.

TAR: (*Rising anger*) Are you trying to tell me the army *didn't* poison my dad?

ANNE: We don't use melodramatic sentences, Mr Al-Turki. What this means is that, unlike those involved with the lawsuit, *your* soil is not, currently, vitally toxic, and so you really have no legal recourse against us.

TAR: I can't fucking believe this.

ANNE: There's no need for that language—

TAR: Do you people ever take responsibility for *anything?!*

ANNE: There is no black and white responsibility here—

TAR: But there's *probability*, isn't there?!

ANNE: I'm not prepared to answer—

TAR: How can you sit there and *say* that?! My father *worked* for you people! He fucking facilitated your whole—he fucking *drove* around the man who sat with Richard Nixon and put an end to the fucking oil embargo! He drove that guy *around*! He was a part of the mechanism, Anne!—of what you do here—

ANNE: Mr Al-Turki—

TAR: —and he ate the tomatoes from the back yard *you* guys buried the weapons in, he ate the fucking tomatoes! He had pulp on his cheek! —And you can't even admit it was chock full of poison? You can't *admit* that? —When the man is on his deathbed with morphine draining into his veins, weighing nintey-five fucking pounds with *shit* dribbling out his ass, and you can't even come fucking clean! *(closer to tears than laughter; and now rage)* It's fucking <u>ridiculous</u>!

(ANNE takes this in.........accepting a portion of it....and then simply watching him closely for a very long moment...)

ANNE: *(Genuine)* I understand what you're going through. *(Beat)* May I ask you a question Mr. Al-Turki? *(Pause)* You come from a decent family, you're educated, you're a good-looking guy. What *happened* to you?

(TAR *looks at* ANNE.)

TAR: I don't know what you're talking about.

ANNE: I'm just asking, in your opinion, what happened?

(TAR *doesn't get where this is headed*)

ANNE: Mr Al-Turki, there's a program we started here last year, a brainstorm, at the Pentagon, that I'd like to share with you. *(Pause)* It's a program to help the youth. Do you like the youth? *(No anwer)* It's a program to help the people of Iraq *like* us better.

(Still no answer)

ANNE: We've sponsored a youth soccer league in Iraq. It's called, "The Iraq Youth Soccer League," and we're looking for able-bodied young, male, role-model types who have both soccer experience and, if we're lucky, some Arabic language skills. Needless to say, you fit both those categories. There are leagues in various towns: Balad, Karbala, Mahmodiyah, Nasir…for Iraqi youth in the ten-to-fifteen year-old range. And so one of the reasons I've called you here today is to offer you a role in this exciting and proactive venture.

(TAR *stands a moment, taking this all in……and then:*)

TAR: Are you fucking nuts?

ANNE: I'm far from nuts.

TAR: Is this your way of trying to shut me up? Make me *join* the team that fucked up my dad?

ANNE: No one did that to your father, Mr Al-Turki—

TAR: The *U S military* did that and now you're saying "if you can't beat us, join us"—all so that I don't fucking *sue* you!

ANNE: Can you calm down a minute?—

TAR: I *am* calm—

ANNE: Good—because I think you should be calm—

TAR: I'm calm as a fucking river, Anne.

ANNE: Good—

TAR: I just happen to think you're *all* liars!

ANNE: Fair enough. *(Calm)* Still, I think you should think about it.

TAR: Why?

ANNE: Because we're not trying to shut you up, what we're *trying* to do is enlist your help, your unique skill set. *(Pause) You're* the one who said you were psyched about what we did to Saddam. My thought was that you might be excited to be part of this venture. A chance for you to put your beliefs into action. Take some responsibiity for your life and the world you live in.

(No answer)

ANNE: Didn't you just say we're all a part of the mechanism? Well I agree: *(Strong)* We're all in this together.

(TAR stands there......as lights find MEL drinking a beer at home, doing nothing, as BOB enters, perhaps from the bedroom. Beats:)

MEL: I'm sorry I left bar the yesterday.

(BOB looks up, taking this in...and then:)

BOB: ...He's not a bad guy, you know. He's *also* dealing with some tough stuff. *(Beat)* And although it seems you might have a thing for Cynthia, he *is* dating her. So it may be more gentlemanly to just, you know, lay low.

MEL: *(Beat)* It's funny...five years ago I was charming.

(BOB's not sure how to respond...so he doesn't.)

MEL: I've been seeing this therapist.

BOB: ...Oh yeah?

MEL: Not romantically, but...I thought you'd wanna know.

BOB: I'm glad.

MEL: It's this thing where you...like...move your eyes back and forth; to dislodge shit.

BOB: ...*Did* it?

MEL: A little bit. *(Beat)* There was this kid I killed over there. *(Looking up)* Did you know that?

BOB: ...I...no, I did not.

MEL: ...And when I went to confirm the kill; afterwards? ...I was still kinda shaking. His body was lying beneath this overpass; where he'd fallen from when I shot him. He was like trying to lay a bomb. *(Pause)* And so I patted him down for weapons and documents. Which there were none. And I was just like, "What are you *doing* here? You're trying to kill Americans 'cause someone told you it was a smart thing to do. But it's *not*. I mean...why'd you make me *do* that?—you fucking dickwad...raghead...haaji fucking...gook.

(Beat; MEL is kind of confused...)

MEL: Sorry. I...I didn't mean gook. *(Beat. A bit neutral)* And...and I was about to leave when I noticed he had an erection. Like ten minutes after I'd shot him. And he still had it. This kid, lying there dead, with an erection. *(Pause)* I guess it's a natural thing. Like losing bowel control. At first I didn't notice it...but then there it was. Pushing out from these pajama things he was wearing. *(Pause)* It was really pathetic.

BOB: ...Yes.

MEL: *(Not mad)* It was really fucking embarrassing. *(Quiet)* That's not what I set out to do, Dad.

(BOB *stands speechless; we see* MEL *register the horror on*
BOB's *face, even as* BOB *tries to conceal it. A moment passes
between them, as we see* BOB *realize that* MEL *has noted his
reaction.)*

MEL: …Maybe I shouldn't have told you.

BOB: No. I'm glad you did.

MEL: No, Dad. You're not glad.

(BOB *and* MEL *regard one another…*BOB *trying to give his
son support.)*

(—*as music fades in and slowly begins to build throughout
the following—*)

(*And lights shift to something altogether new……*)

(*…finding us inside* TAR's *childhood home, where we
eventually see the body of his father [as represented by the
actor who plays* BOB], *prone on a bench. Nearby,* TAR *holds
a bottle of tequila and speaks aloud, as though perhaps
leaving a message from a cell phone.)*

TAR: Hey Cynthia, it's me, thinking of you. I just ate
a tequila worm. *(Beat)* I gotta talk to you, Cynth. Too
much shit pilin' up on me. It's fucking…loop-de-
loop…

(*During the following,* TAR, *still speaking to* CYNTH, *stands
and goes to his father's body, where he goes through the
ritualistic motions of cleaning the body, at the end of which
he closes the eylids and kisses the forehead.)*

TAR: Biyigghrak bi kubbayet my. My Mom used to
have this saying, that she'd always tell me, when I
was a kid. "Nuhtaem billadi yuhtemina." It basically
means, "You take care of those who took care of you."
It's something we do. It's what I've *done*, Cynth. Stayed
with him. Fought for him. Everything except….speak
better Arabic. And marry a Saudi. Eed Wihdeh Ma Bit
Zakkif. And then it's gone and you're like…you wish

you *did* speak more. 'Cause suddenly there's no one left to talk to. You wake up and...everything that was home...is gone. Just a big 'ole pile of dirt. And you're standing there by yourself on top of it, trying to figure out what happened.

(TAR's *phone call has been overlapped by* MEL, *who is doing push-ups, and now begins singing softly, a can of Coors Light balanced on his back.*)

MEL:
I love rock and roll
Put another dime in the jukebox, baby

(—*as* TAR, *still leaving his message, finds a straw, puts it in the mouth of the tequila bottle and tips it until he can take a large sip...*)

TAR: I kinda wish you were on top of me here, empowering yourself as a woman of the Twenty-first Century. Seriously. You're like the only one I can talk to. We both like mashed potatoes. I love you. Thanks for taking me serious.

MEL: I love rock and roll

TAR: *(Still into phone)* P S. My dad died this afternoon. I wasn't even in the room.

(MEL *stops the push-ups...*)

TAR: *(Still into phone)* Where *are* you?

(MEL *sits straight now, a small pill in his hand, holding it up to a light, looking at it with one eye closed. After a moment, he swallows it, chasing it with Coors.*)

(TAR *has shut the phone and begins to undress down to his tighty-whitey's, softly, slowly singing*)

TAR:
As I was digging, in my backyard
I found some fucking chem-i-cal weapons
So I found an oozie, and went to the Pentagon

And shot the chick there, even though she's hot
And now I'm drunk as, a fucking asshole—

(TAR *is cut off by the distant sounds of an Arabic lullaby,*
soft, reverberating, growing. He stops, listening.........
but then it fades......as we now hear MEL, *on Ecstasy,*
beautifully trance-like, quietly singing—)

MEL:
I love hearts and minds
Stick a plastic fork in the entire country
I love hearts and minds
Spread some democracy across my ass...

(*As a sudden, single light finds* CHUCK, [*played by* BOB]
with a handheld mike, mid-speech—)

CHUCK: When soldiers prepare for battle, they
determine their geometry of fire. It's a strategy for
defense; fire support coordination measures; basically
so they don't shoot each other. (*Pause*) But the thing
about these wars like the one in Iraq, like a war against
any insurgency, is that they're fought on asymmetrical
battlefields. Which is to say—as we all now know—
they're not conventional war scenarios, you're not
fighting guys in "red coats" standing with their guns
on the far side of a field. There's no logic to the whole
thing, no predictability, no linearity. It basically just
means they're coming at you from every which fucking
way. (*Beat*) Which is, of course, the point. About
everything. Everywhere. In life. It comes at you. Life
comes *at* you.

(*We find* MEL, *in his own light, standing. He lights a*
cigarette...)

CHUCK: You're standing in a newly-paved parking lot
on the banks of the glorious Euphrates river, smoking
the day's last cigarette and thinking about the Michael
Bay D V D you're gonna watch on your laptop that
night. The stars are out, just like they've been over that

river for a million years, and little do you know that
some pissed-off Iraqi teenager's got you in his scope,
the scope of the gun he took from the body of a marine
marksman he'd snuck up on and stabbed with a steak
knife. And this kid hates you 'cause of what you've
done to his cousin and his country and his pride.
And he's got you in his cross-hairs on a glorious Iraqi
night. It's an extremely intimate scenario. Exquisitely
intimate.

(Light up on TAR, *who during the preceding has knelt into a
a sniper's pose, imaginary rifle aimed at* MEL, *who continues
to smoke, staring out...)*

CHUCK: And what does one do to fight that? *Is*
there a logic? a path home? a geometry of fire to
defend against that cycle of death you're about to
become a part of, on this bizarrely asymmetrical
battlefield? *(Beat)* Well—if there is, it's to be found
in our imagination. We have to use our *will.* Like
that paralyzed fellow *willing* the computer curser
with nothing but the pure power of intention.
(Pause) We have to change consciousness, folks. We
have to become willing participants in a profound
transformation of human consciousness. *(Pause)* Can
we do it? Can we change the geometry *within*...and in
so doing, the geometry of the *world*?

*(*TAR *turns out, away from* MEL.*)*

CHUCK: Well the answer is yes.

(Sudden shift of lights—early morning; MEL *is standing in
a field of tall reed grass......where across the way is an* ARAB
KID, *played by the actor who plays* TAR. *Silence... [When
the* KID *talks, it's pretty much the way* TAR *talks, although
perhaps a bit younger and with a slight accent])*

MEL: Hey.

KID: *(Beat)* Hey.

MEL: …You live around here?

KID: Yeah.

MEL: Mahmoudiyah?

KID: Nasir.

MEL: Is that nice?

KID: …No.

MEL: Right. *(Beat)* My name's Mel.

KID: Sayeed.

MEL: Hey, Sayeed.

KID: What about you?

MEL: What do you mean?

KID: Where do *you* live?

MEL: Northern Virginia.

KID: Arlington?

MEL: Fairfax.

KID: Nice.

MEL: *(Beat)* I wanted to…

KID: What?

MEL: Talk to you.

KID: About what?

MEL: About the time I shot you in the head.

(The KID *just takes this in)*

MEL: On Highway One. South of Baghdad.

KID: I remember.

MEL: So…can we talk?

KID: Why? Make yourself feel better?

MEL: Yeah.

KID: Is it working?

MEL: No.

*(Beat...*MEL *not sure what to say next; and then:)*

MEL: Are your parents...?

KID: Are they what?

MEL: Okay. Are they okay?

KID: No.

MEL: What are...are they—?

KID: Very disappointed; my father...is very disappointed.

MEL: What does he say?

KID: He says Fuck You. He says he hopes you die. He says you are fuck. Fuck you. You wanted to do good, but you are shit. You are shit. You are fuck. You are shit-fuck. You will die unhappy forever and ever. And you deserve it. Fuck you. *(Beat)* That is what he says.

(Silence; MEL *absorbs, at a loss...)*

MEL: Did you play sports, Sayeed?

KID: Yeah. Soccer. *(Pause)* Me and my cousin, we were very good.

MEL: Oh yeah?

KID: Yeah. Very fast. Very tricky. My cousin, *he* will keep playing, I hope.

MEL: I like soccer.

KID: You wanna play?

MEL: Now?

KID: Yeah.

MEL: It's hard.

KID: Why?

MEL: I'm on a serious amount of Ecstasy. *(Pause)* It helps with stress.

KID: *"Post Traumatic"* Stress?

MEL: Yeah.

KID: "P T S D"?

MEL: Yeah.

KID: Sounds nifty.

MEL: Yeah. *(Pause)* It helps you…re-imagine things.

KID: Totally.

MEL: Chemicals are our friends.

KID: Gotcha.

(KID *and* MEL *stand in silence a moment.)*

MEL: How old are you, Sayeed?

KID: Fourteen. Almost

(MEL *is forced to take this in a moment)*

MEL: *(Beat)* Can I tell you something?

KID: Sure.

MEL: *(Pause)* That day. When you died. I came up to you. And I stood on your face. With my full weight. Which is… *(Shakes head a little)* I stood on the front of your head. On which there was no back. *(Pause)* And Sayeed?

KID: Yes?

MEL: Your head?

KID: Yes?

MEL: It caved in. It totally collapsed under my foot. Like a fucking…lantern. And your brains were like gravy…coming out of a broken lantern.

KID: *(Pause)* Why did you do that?

MEL: …I think I…I'd heard about how in Vietnam a kill couldn't be confirmed until you physically put your foot *on* the body. And so…I don't know why…but I did that. To you. *(Beat)* I guess I was trying to show off for the guys. *(Pause)* And it musta worked; 'cause a couple of them laughed. *(Beat)* Did you know that?

KID: *(Pause)* No.

MEL: ...I didn't think so. *(Pause)* I don't think I remembered it either...'til a couple minutes ago.

KID: Mind games.

MEL: I guess. *(Pause)* I fucked up, Sayeed. And I just wanted to say...I'm sorry. *(Beat—looking at him directly—near whisper:)* I'm sorry.

KID: I'm getting that.

(Silence)

MEL: I'd like to...you know...make it up to...at least to, like, your parents.

KID: That's a long shot, Mel.

MEL: I know. But do you have any idea how I might try?

KID: To make it up to my Dad?

MEL: Yeah.

KID: No.

MEL: *(Pause)* Nothing?

(KID thinks for a moment...)

KID: Exude positive energy? *(Pause)* Self-actualize at the highest level. *(Casual)* Live better.

(MEL considers this with all seriousness....)

KID: Would you like to hug, Mel?

MEL: ...I don't know. Do you think that would...?

KID: Probably not. *(Pause)* No. *(Definitive:)* No.

MEL: Right. *(Beat...)* Okay, man.

KID: Okay, man.

MEL: Bye.

KID: Bye.

(KID *and* MEL *regard one another for a moment...and then the* KID *turns away*)

(MEL *stands; stillness...*)

(*After a moment,* TAR *perhaps walks by. This is both literal and not literal, in that* MEL *senses him walk by as much as he actually sees him....*)

(*Sound of cell phone ringing...*)

(*...as light finds* MEL *sitting at the bar, lost in thought, almost as though he's still with Sayeed.* CYNTH *is behind the bar counter; she checks the caller I D on her phone...and decides to not answer. The phone stops ringing and for a long moment there is just silence. Finally,* MEL *looks up.*)

MEL: I took some ecstacy last night.

CYNTH: ...Why?

MEL: I heard about a clinical trial where they give it to trauma victims for their stress, so...I self-administered.

CYNTH: ...Was it fun?

MEL: It was all right. (*Pause*) You're supposed to take it in a controlled environment, and the doctor stays with you the whole time, talks you through your traumatic event...and then has sex with you.

CYNTH: You're lying.

MEL: It's the love drug. It's a great perk.

CYNTH: I see. And what was *your* traumatic event?

MEL: Not being able to date you.

(CYNTH *and* MEL *watch each other.*)

MEL: I'm not a bad guy, you know.

CYNTH: I know.

MEL: Seriously. I bathe a lot. And I'm thorough. I get every crevice.

(CYNTH *smiles a little.*)

CYNTH: You doing okay? These days?

MEL: I'm doing okay.

CYNTH: You *look* better.

MEL: Are you saying I look *good?*

CYNTH: *(A smile)* Yes, you look good.

MEL: *You* look……fucking exquisite.

CYNTH: …Thank you.

MEL: We should seriously be going steady.

CYNTH: *(Beat)* I'm actually thinking about taking off for a couple months.

MEL: Taking off where?

CYNTH: Away. Sacramento.

MEL: *Why?*

CYNTH: I have a friend who makes documentaries. She asked me to come out and help.

MEL: So you're leaving for *good?*

CYNTH: It's just something I'm thinking about.

(—*as we hear sound of a flush, followed a moment later by* BOB *exiting the bar's bathroom*)

BOB: That's a very nice bathroom you have there, Cynthia.

CYNTH: Yeah?

BOB: Yeah. Very nice. Very soothing.

CYNTH: Good.

BOB: Did Mel tell you I'm taking him out to dinner?

CYNTH: No—

BOB: To celebrate his job interview.

CYNTH: *(To* MEL*)* You didn't tell me that—

BOB: Which apparently went very well.

CYNTH: What kind of job?

MEL: Gatekeeper of Doom.

BOB: I have a cousin who runs an investment firm.

MEL: *(To* CYNTH*)* It's called "The Hitler Youth".

CYNTH: *(To* BOB*)* You must be happy.

BOB: I'm happy he's feeling better.

MEL: Speaking of which, Dad—don't you think Cynthia and I should be together?

BOB: Not for me to say, Mel—

MEL: I mean, c'mon: Look at us.

(MEL *puts his arm around* CYNTH—*as she realizes that* TAR *is standing there; it's not clear whether he's heard the end of their conversation.)*

CYNTH: Hey.

TAR: Hey.

BOB: Hey, T-Bone!

TAR: Hi, Bob. *(He takes a few steps in)* What's up?

CYNTH: Not much. …You okay?

TAR: Yeah.

CYNTH: What's up?

TAR: I've been calling; I need to talk.

CYNTH: Sure.

TAR: Did you get my messages?

CYNTH: No. I mean—you only left one but I didn't—

TAR: You didn't listen to it?

CYNTH: I couldn't understand it. You were totally drunk.

TAR: But did you *hear* it?

CYNTH: Not all of it; no.

MEL: What's up, T-Bone?

TAR: What's up.

MEL: Not much.

TAR: ...We seem to keep meeting here.

MEL: It's my home away from home.

TAR: *(Re: the door)* So can we—?

MEL: Can she serve us one more round?

BOB: We should get going, Mel.

MEL: We will, I just wanna get one more round. It's like a good-bye party.

BOB: ...T-Bone? Will you join us?

TAR: No thanks.

MEL: C'mon, T-Boy, join us for a drink.

TAR: ...That's really all right.

MEL: Well don't take her away from us, man, it might be our last chance. *(To* CYNTH*)* Can we get some shots? Jim Beam?

BOB: I'm not drinking whiskey, Mel.

MEL: Fine, Tequila. You do tequila, Cynthia—

CYNTH: I do.

MEL: Three shots of tequila; T-Bone? *(No answer)* C'mon—one drink. To make up for my not joining you last time.

TAR: *(With an almost resigned smile)* ...Fine.

MEL: Four tequila's, Cynthia!

(Silence as CYNTH *pours drinks.)*

BOB: So how's it been hanging, T-Bone?

TAR: It's fine.

BOB: Good.

MEL: *(Beat; to* TAR*)* So you come here a lot?

TAR: Yeah.

MEL: Oh, that's right. You two...

TAR: Yeah. *(Beat)* You too, I guess.

MEL: Yeah, I live up the street. It's a great bar.

TAR: ...Why?

*(*MEL *looks from* TAR *to* CYNTH, *then back to* TAR...*)*

MEL: 'Cause I like it here.

TAR: *Why?*

MEL: ...Great decor.

BOB: It's true. *(To* TAR*)* Have you checked out the bathroom?

MEL: *(To* TAR*)* I'm just fucking around, man.

(But TAR's *not laughing)*

CYNTH: Tariq?

TAR: Yeah?

CYNTH: Can you chill out?

TAR: I'm totally chill.

(Beat—as TAR *looks from* CYNTH, *to* MEL*)*

TAR: I'm just wondering what's going on.

CYNTH: There's nothing's going on—

TAR: I feel like there is.

CYNTH: There's not.

TAR: Can you tell me the truth?

MEL: What is he *talking* about?

TAR: *(Direct)* I get tired of people fucking with me.

MEL: You don't *own* her, man.

BOB: Let's just sip our beers, guys.

(BOB sips his beer; silence…)

TAR: *(To MEL)* Are you trying to disrespect me?

MEL: Who is this guy, Charles Bronson?

TAR: *(Strong)* I'm telling you not to disrespect me.

BOB: Whattayou say we settle down, T-Bone—

TAR: *(Still to MEL)* Do you understand what I'm saying?

MEL: I understand that you're a freak—

TAR: Shut up.

CYNTH: *Tariq*—

TAR: *(To her)* No, every time I come in here this guy is here acting like an entitled jerk-

CYNTH: He's not a jerk.

TAR: *What?*

CYNTH: He's not a jerk.

MEL: I'm not a jerk—

TAR: Of *course* he's a jerk, he's a marine!

CYNTH: *(To TAR)* Let's go outside—

(TAR steps toward MEL—)

TAR: Do *not* mess with me today.

BOB: Okay, let's just sit down and talk this out.

TAR: There's nothing to talk about, he's playing fucking games!

MEL: *What?*

TAR: *(Loud and clear)* Stay away from my girlfriend!

MEL: Oh *Jesus*—

CYNTH: Tariq—

TAR: What?

CYNTH: This isn't even *about* me.

TAR: Sure it is—

CYNTH: No, because there's nothing going on.

MEL: Exactly, she's a lovely woman—

BOB: *Mel*—

TAR: *(To* MEL*)* What's your problem? —You don't like me?—

MEL: I like you fine—

TAR: You think you're some higher-than-thou marine fuck-all who can go around treating people like shit?!

BOB: Enough, T-Bone—

TAR: He's doing it on purpose, Bob—

MEL: Doing *what*?

CYNTH: You *have* to calm down, Tariq—

TAR: I'm tired of people fucking with me, especially this little *dickwad* here!

*(*MEL *is up, poised and in* TAR's *face; strong.)*

MEL: Watch what you fuckin' say to me.

*(*MEL *turns and leaves; silence…)*

BOB: T-Bone, whatever's going on here, this is not the way to handle this.

TAR: I *haven't* handled it yet, Bob, I'm just trying to get some answers.

CYNTH: I don't know what answers you're talking about.

TAR: *(Looking at her)* No?

CYNTH: No. You're acting like a complete jerk.

(Silence in the room)

BOB: *(Gentle)* T-Bone. Tariq. I think you're misunderstanding things here in a very serious way.

TAR: No I'm not.

CYNTH: *(Pause; trying to change subject)* Did you visit your Dad last night?

TAR: Did I visit my Dad? *(Pause)* Yeah. I did.

(—and then MEL *suddenly walks back in carrying a 9MM Glock revolver; he calmly sits at his bar stool and places it on the bar in front of him.)*

MEL: This is just in case you decide to bug me anymore.

BOB: ......Put that fucking thing away.

MEL: Not until he calms down.

BOB: This is *no* way to—

MEL: He walked in here and he started talking shit, he looks like a psycho and I'm not just gonna sit here and take it.

TAR: *(Beat)* This how you handle it in the Marines? This what you did in Iraq?

CYNTH: Tariq—

TAR: Pull your gun out every time someone challenged you on the truth?

MEL: Fuck off—

TAR: Fuck off yourself you fuckin' *G I-Joe fucking Nazi!*

BOB: ...Okay, Mel, I really think we should leave now.

MEL: I'm not leaving—

BOB: Yes you are—

MEL: It's a free country.

BOB: Then put the goddam gun away!

MEL: No.

BOB: Fine, then give it to me—

MEL: What is it—you don't trust me?

BOB: Of course I do—

MEL: I thought you thought I was better—

BOB: I do—

MEL: Well maybe you don't—

BOB: Listen—

MEL: Why is that, Dad?

BOB: It's not true—

MEL: Why *is* that?—

BOB: Because you're *not* better. Obviously. *(Pause; calmer)* Nobody gets better overnight. *(Pause)* So just do what I'm asking.

MEL: *No!*

(Silence in the room...... After a long moment TAR speaks to MEL in a low voice, eventually slowly approaching him.)

TAR: You like being a military guy?

CYNTH: *(To TAR)* You're acting incredibly stupid.

TAR: Yeah.

BOB: T-Bone—

TAR: *(To MEL)* Mess up people's lives?

CYNTH: Can you stop?

TAR: No.

CYNTH: Why?

TAR: Because. *(He speaks to* MEL, *almost hushed)* Kill a buncha of Arabs then come back home and act like an asshole? Is that sorta your thing?—

BOB: Tariq, that's enough.

TAR: "Mel"? *(No answer)* You're not gonna answer me? You're fine to kill Iraqi kids but you can't have a conversation with me? Here in your little bar? Where you don't have to deal with all the bodies back over there in "haaji land"?

CYNTH: Tariq, let's go outside.

TAR: *(Incredibly quiet but intense)* You have no *idea* the damage you caused. *(Pause)* Over there you're a killer but here you're a king? *(Pause)* Is that what gets you off? Big guy? 'Cause you don't have to think about all those little *kids*?—

(In one swift move MEL *has raised the gun to* TAR's *head. He holds it steady, three feet from* TAR's *skull. Silence)*

MEL: Shut the fuck up.

TAR: ...Sure—

MEL: *Shut up.*

BOB: ...Mel, *please, please* lower that. *(No answer) Please. (Silence) Mel.*

(Silence...)

(Single light finds MEL *as he turns, gun still raised to* TAR's *head, and speaks to us:)*

MEL: I can't really describe what it's like to kill. All I can say is that it seems to be a place where...where you recognize...complete indifference. Where you understand, with clarity, that nature...in all its beauty, really doesn't give a shit. At *all. (He lowers the gun and turns to us more fully...)* I imagine it's the same as *being* killed. Like when you turn the gun on yourself....and save everyone a lot of trouble. *(Pause)* I don't think I

would mind nature's indifference to my *own* death
because I probably, in some very direct, karmic way,
deserve it. *(Pause)* I *do* care, however, that nature seems
ambivalent about my *having* killed. Because for me…
no matter what I do, I still think about you every
day. *(Pause)* Sayeed. *(Pause)* *All* the time. *(Pause)* Your
image; your ripped-off face; your caved-in brains…
your ripped-off life. *(Pause)* It's my image…it's my
fault. And there *is* no forgiveness. *(Beat; more to us:)*
There are things we can control; through science or
whatever. And then there are things we can't. One
minute we're *exquisite* in our control; we display grace
and precision in our agency over even the tiniest of our
actions. And the next minute…it's like it's anybody's
fucking guess. *(Pause)* I dunno. *(He turns back to*
TAR, *again raising the gun. Beat—and then he speaks to
us again:)* I honestly love life. I do. *(Now lowering the
gun)* And even though I'm not very good at it, I try
to remind myself that we're all a part of it. *(Pause)*
Because we *are, all*…responsible.

(Blackout)

END OF PLAY

www.ingramcontent.com/pod-product-compliance
Lightning Source LLC
Chambersburg PA
CBHW060305100426
42742CB00011B/1875